George McCoy Musgrave

Competitive Debate

RULES AND TECHNIQUES

Third edition

808.5
M97c

THE H. W. WILSON COMPANY
New York   1957

First Edition 1945

Revised Edition 1946
Second Printing 1948

Third Edition 1957

Printed in the United States of America

Library of Congress Catalog Card No. 57-5421

PREFACE

The purpose of this book is to summarize for the debater, coach, and judge the accepted practices of debate. Consideration has been given both the elementary techniques that every neophyte should learn at once, and the advanced techniques which should not be attempted until after a thorough groundwork has been laid. Major emphasis has been placed on those items of greatest concern to the participant in preparing for next week's debate; background and theory have been carefully presented in other publications (see bibliography), and that material is not repeated.

Accordingly, perhaps a summary here of the conception of debating on which the present work is based would not be out of place. Debate, to me, is essentially an *educational* process; its justification in high school and college lies in the training it gives the participants. Debate *may* provide the answers to national problems, and it *may* convert the public to the "right" side of the questions discussed, but primarily its purpose is the personal development of the participants; other results are secondary.

From the debater's point of view, debate is a highly enjoyable mental sport. Most debaters do not go out for debate to improve their thought processes any more than football players go out for football to strengthen their muscles. Both participate in their respective sports because they enjoy them. Of course, there are other incentives. High school or college credit is often given the debater, and financial support is often given the football player. But the educator must recognize that even though debate develops the participants in a beneficial manner, the debater has other incentives which to him may be just as important or more so. One of the most important of these is the feeling of personal enjoyment.

Debate, like almost every form of human activity, is competitive. Competition can no more be eliminated from debate or discussion or any other speech activity than it can be eliminated from the world in which the debater finds himself after graduation. Nor is it desirable that debate competition be eliminated or reduced; rather, it should be encouraged, both as an approach to post-graduation activities and as a means of stimulating work of a higher quality. Again and again it has been demonstrated that the educational benefits of debate are greatest in an atmosphere where each student, through competition, is spurred on to his best efforts and highest achievements.

Debate is a speech activity; that is, it is oral in form and is usually administered, on the college level, by the Department of Speech. This has led a few into paying as much attention to diction and gestures as to what the speakers are saying. Only when one realizes that the main purpose of the speaker is to communicate ideas, and that devices of effective speech are useful only to the extent that they aid this process, can such devices be evaluated properly. The debate judge gives the decision to the team doing what the proposition requires; delivery affects the decision, but only to the extent that delivery aids or hinders the debater in meeting the requirements of the proposition.

The three possible contributions of this book which concern me most are (1) the codification of rules, (2) the method of case organization, and (3) the method of judging.

The codification of rules is one of the jobs that first prompted me to prepare the manuscript. For many years debaters, coaches, and judges have had to learn the "ropes" the hard way—from trial and error, from the painful experience of making mistakes and discovering them too late. In all other competitive sports the participants have the opportunity to read the rule book from the very beginning; they are not required to fumble around in the dark learning the rules by observation, perhaps reaching incorrect conclusions. Apparently no comprehensive set of rules of debate has ever been published; it was to meet this situation that Chapter 1 was written.

The method of case organization suggested is purely optional on the part of the debaters—but the teams which developed it maintained such consistently good records over a period of years that I think it worthy of careful consideration.

The quality of judging has always been a sore point, and unnecessarily so. What is needed is an objective and easily applied technique of judging, one which answers the question, "Which team did what the proposition requires?" The double-summary technique is offered as such a procedure.

This edition (the third) has been largely rewritten, with new material, based on observations and suggestions accumulated since the previous edition. Some of the more significant changes are the recodification of rules, the expanded material on cross examination, the simplified approach to case organization and judging, the new chapter on administration, the appendix listing national topics and national tournament winners, and the new annotated bibliography.

As in earlier editions, I would like to acknowledge my debt to Blake S. Root, formerly coach of debate at Western High School, Washington, D.C.; Glenn H. Leggett, formerly coach of debate at the Massachusetts Institute of Technology; and E. R. Nichols, formerly head of the Department of Speech, University of Redlands, for much valuable guidance in previous years.

Appreciation is due Bower Aly, Edward Betz, Waldo Braden, Paul Carmack, Oliver Carpenter, Lionel Crocker, Cadet Richard P. Dowell, Harold Gibson, Hugo Hellman, Robert S. Henry, Bruno Jacob, Glenn Jones, Toshio Kanchi, Emmett Long, D. J. Nabors, E. R. Nichols, Larry Norton, Gregg Phifer, Victor Powell, Brooks Quimby, Forrest Rose, Robert Scott, J. Weston Walch, and the publishers of the material listed in the bibliography, for help in gathering information for the present edition.

It is hoped that the information presented will prove useful to debaters, coaches, and judges who desire to improve the caliber of their work through an understanding of the procedures and techniques used by others.

GEORGE McCOY MUSGRAVE

Toledo
September 1956

CONTENTS

CONTENTS

CONTENTS

1

RULES OF DEBATE

Debate, like many competitive activities, has rules and customs with which participants and judges should be thoroughly familiar. Until 1945, the rules were largely unwritten; they passed by word of mouth from debater to debater and from school to school. It is not surprising, then, to find some disagreement as to what they actually are.

In the last few years considerable progress has been made in the development of standards and procedures generally acceptable on a national basis. Widespread intersectional competition and national debate publications have accelerated this trend.

Those principles which seem inherently sound, and which meet with fairly wide acceptance in high school and college debating, are included in this chapter as "rules." Other practices, less widely recognized or more arbitrary in nature, appear as "customs" in other chapters.

THE TEAMS

The rules governing participants are these:

Rule 1. *There are two teams. Each team consists of two or three speakers.*

When the debate is arranged, agreement is reached as to whether two- or three-man teams will be employed. Two-man teams now predominate to such an extent that in cases where no mention is made of the number of debaters, it is generally safe to assume that two-man teams are intended.

THE SPEECHES

Rule 2 a. *The speeches and speaking time are divided equally between the two teams.*

The tournament rules or debate contract specifies the amount of time allocated to each speech. The total speaking time generally runs about one hour, including questioning periods.

Rule 2 b. *Each team has two or three constructive speeches.*

It is customary for each member of the team to be allowed one constructive speech. Thus, if two-man teams are employed, there are two constructive speeches per team. If three-man teams are employed, there are three constructive speeches per team.

Rule 2 c. *Each team has from one to three rebuttal speeches.*

In standard debate, it is customary for each participant to speak in rebuttal. In Oregon [1] debate, each participant may speak in rebuttal, or sometimes there is only one rebuttal for the team. The number of rebuttal speeches is, of course, specified in the pre-debate correspondence or tournament rules.

Rule 2 d. *The affirmative gives the first constructive speech, and the constructive speeches alternate: affirmative, negative, affirmative, negative.*

Rule 2 e. *The negative gives the first rebuttal speech, and the rebuttals alternate: negative, affirmative, negative, affirmative.*

Thus, the affirmative has both the first and last speeches of the debate. This arrangement is designed to compensate for the affirmative's burden of proof, explained later.

Rule 2 f. *In Oregon type debate, each team has one or more questioning periods, in addition to the constructive speeches and rebuttals.*

[1] The term "Oregon debate," as employed in this book, denotes any form of cross-examination debate. The name comes from the University of Oregon, where it originated.

There are several versions of cross-examination debate. The arrangement to be used is agreed upon when the debate is being planned.

THE TOPIC

When the topic is worded, whether by the national committee or by the local debaters, the following rule is applied:

Rule 3 a. *When worded as a proposition of policy, the topic requires the affirmative to support some specified action by some particular individual or group.*

The proposition of policy takes the form, "Resolved, that the United States should grant statehood to Hawaii." Other wordings are possible and have been used in the past, but they have proved less satisfactory. The national high school and the national college topics have been phrased in this manner for so many years that other wordings are now generally considered improper except for international debate. The material in this book is based on the presumption that the topic is worded as a proposition of policy.

Of course, there are other requirements for a good topic. It should be interesting, clear, have one central idea, and not be one-sided. But even if these requirements are not met, it can still be debated; such requirements must be considered matters of good technique rather than rules.

Occasionally a contest hinges on the definition of a word or phrase in the topic. The rule is this:

Rule 3 b. *The affirmative has the right to make any reasonable definition of each of the terms of the proposition.*

A "reasonable" definition generally means the definition intended when the proposition was phrased, or the technical definition of the term as used by professionals in that field. If the affirmative's definition is not reasonable, the negative should challenge it at the earliest opportunity.

Rule 3 c. *If the negative challenges the reasonableness of a definition by the affirmative, the judge must accept* *the definition of the team that shows better grounds for its interpretation of the term.*

The judge is not expected to exercise his own taste in the matter, but to listen to the evidence and logic of the teams and to support the definition shown to be more reasonable.

Rule 3 d. *Once the negative has accepted the affirmative's definitions, it may not later object to them, even though it later develops that they are unreasonable. Failure of the negative to object to the affirmative's definitions in the first constructive speech following the definitions is equivalent to acceptance of them by the negative.*

If the negative wishes to quarrel with the affirmative's interpretation of the topic, it must do so at once. Otherwise the debate might literally be half over before the teams have decided what they are arguing about. If the negative, through oversight, accepts or fails to object to an unreasonable definition by the affirmative, it should not later be heard objecting that the definition was unreasonable.

"Trick" definitions are not encouraged. Unusual definitions are sometimes employed successfully by getting the negative to agree that they are reasonable before it realizes that they are not, but since strategic cases are always possible without resorting to such definitions, it is better to avoid them. They lead only to bickering and quibbling.

One practice, which has much to commend it, is for the two teams to agree on the definitions of any controversial terms in their pre-debate correspondence. These definitions are then included in the debate contract or tournament rules, and are announced by the chairman at the start of the contest.

Of course, all this does not mean that either team is required to define formally any term of the proposition. High school debaters do seem to prefer formal definitions, picking out the terms one by one ("By federal government, we mean . . ."). College debaters, on the other hand, often prefer to define the entire proposition by explaining the plan they are supporting. Either method is, of course, appropriate in either high school or college work.

The old argument about the meaning of the word "should" in the proposition still arises. Here is the generally accepted definition:

Rule 3 e. *The phrase "should adopt" or its equivalent means that the affirmative must show that the plan, if adopted, would be desirable. It does not in any way obligate the affirmative to show that the necessary approvals could be obtained.*

For example, the constitutionality of the proposal is irrelevant; it must be presumed that the Constitution could be so amended if necessary. Similarly, the claim that too many voters or too many members of Congress are opposed to the bill for it to pass is irrelevant; the only question to be settled is whether or not the plan would be desirable if adopted.[2]

On the other hand, the negative may choose to claim that the plan is not practicable—that if it were put into effect it would not work, either immediately or at some future date. The plan certainly wouldn't be desirable if it didn't work, so this is a legitimate negative case which the affirmative must meet.

Rule 3 f. *The phrase "should adopt" or its equivalent obligates the affirmative to recommend that action be taken in the reasonably near future.*

Ordinarily, no time limit is specified in the topic. Nevertheless, one is implied. The affirmative may allow a reasonable amount of time for working out the details and establishing the administrative functions, but delay until condi-

[2] See F. W. Lambertson's "The Meaning of the Word 'Should' in a Question of Policy," *Quarterly Journal of Speech*, 28:421-4, December 1942. An abstract of this article will be found in the bibliography, Appendix D.

tions have changed in some significant respect, or until (say) Great Britain tries the plan first, is not permissible.

If no such requirement as this existed, the affirmative might recommend that action be taken twenty years from now, when the plan could be adopted under highly favorable circumstances. The negative's position could be identical, and no debate would ensue. Therefore, the affirmative must support reasonably prompt action.

POSITIONS OF THE TEAMS

Sometimes the right of a team to recommend certain action is challenged. The limitations are not severe, but they should be clearly understood.

Rule 4 a. *The affirmative must advocate everything required by the topic itself.*

If the affirmative fails to meet all of the requirements of the proposition, it fails in its burden of proof and consequently must lose the debate.

Rule 4 b. *The affirmative may work out the details of its plan as it sees fit. It may take on the burden of proving anything else it desires.*

Of course, the more the affirmative advocates, the more it must prove, so the usual technique is to recommend as little as possible. However, if the affirmative does wish to recommend and support more than is required of it by the topic, the negative has no right to object. The affirmative is assuming the burden of proof for the entire enlarged plan, and if it fails to meet this responsibility, the negative wins.

Rule 4 c. *The negative may offer any counterplan that would be in order in a legislative assembly discussing the proposition.*

The ideal counterplan is one that offers some change in principle from the affirmative proposal, and gives sufficient grounds for rejecting the affirmative proposal.[3] The counterplan actually offered, however, may be something less than ideal, and therefore it is important that each participant clearly understand what is permissible and what is not.

A counterplan which closely parallels the affirmative recommendation, differing only in minor respects, is adequate only if the negative shows that the difference between the two is so important that the affirmative plan should be rejected in favor of the negative proposal.

A counterplan based on surprise may, if successful, catch the affirmative unprepared. In the moment of anguish that comes when the affirmative realizes that it has no answer, there may be charges that the negative proposal is out of order. Actually, surprise in itself is perfectly legitimate. No proposal is ever out of order simply because it was not anticipated by the opposition.

Facetious and irrelevant counterplans are clearly out of order. Such plans would be useless in any event because they would not give logical grounds for rejecting the resolution.

Following legislative practice,[4] disputed matter is admitted if there is doubt as to its admissibility.

Rule 4 d. *The affirmative must explain, upon demand by the negative, the major features and policies under which the proposed plan is to operate. If the negative recommends a counterplan, it has the same duty.*

Neither team may leave its plan so vague as to prevent a reasonable attack by the opposition on grounds of practicability. For instance, when advocating a federal union of the nations of Europe, the affirmative, upon demand, must explain the basis for the selection of representatives from member countries—that is, population, area, natural resources, literate population, or other method.

On the other hand, there is no obligation to explain minor details. The affirmative does not have to know how many

[3] Discussed by F. W. Lambertson in "Plan and Counterplan in a Question of Policy," *Quarterly Journal of Speech,* 29:48-52, February 1943.

[4] Henry M. Robert, *Rules of Order Revised* (Chicago, Scott, Foresman and Company, 1951), p. 146.

representatives Luxembourg will have, so long as it explains the basis of Luxembourg's representation. If the negative can show that the decision of the affirmative about an apparently minor detail of the plan is vitally important, then the affirmative must explain how that part of its plan will work; but if the negative attack is of the "hit-and-run" variety, the affirmative is under no obligation to answer each of these minor objections.

Sometimes an affirmative team decides to leave as much as possible to a commission or legislative body to decide so that the negative will have limited grounds on which to attack. This is permissible with regard to minor details, but if the negative demands an explanation of the major features of the plan, the affirmative is obligated to provide it.

Once a team has made known its position on major or minor issues, or even on small details, it is governed by the following rule:

Rule 4 e. *No revision of position of a team is permitted during the debate.*

This rule is designed to prevent teams from wriggling out of contradictions between speakers by simply saying that they had revised their attitude in the meantime. Furthermore, it simplifies the proceedings and enables everyone concerned to follow the debate more easily; one can readily visualize the difficulty in pinning anyone down if speakers were permitted to shift their position whenever they chose.

When a team shifts ground on some issue, the judge should consider the point won by the opposing team. The only exception would be made when the revision is relatively minor and when, except for the shift of ground, the team making the point has a clearcut superiority on that particular issue.

PROOF

A great deal has been written and said about the burden of proof, and certain misconceptions have arisen about the duty of the affirmative. The rule is simple:

Rule 5 a. *He who asserts must prove.*

This principle applies equally to the two teams. Of course, the affirmative must show that its plan is desirable, which means that it must show that some benefits will result; otherwise it has failed to give reason for adopting the plan, and has lost the debate. The commonly heard statement that "the affirmative has the burden of proof" means that and nothing more.

On the other hand, if the negative wants the judge and audience to accept the idea that there are certain defects which outweigh the plan's good points, then it must assume the burden of proving that such disadvantages actually will result.

If the negative introduces a counterplan, it has the burden of showing how it is better than the affirmative's proposal; the affirmative then has the duty of establishing any alleged objections to the counterplan. In every instance, he who asserts must prove.

Rule 5 b. *In order to establish an assertion, the team must support it with enough evidence and logic to convince an intelligent but previously uninformed person that it is more reasonable to believe the assertion than to disbelieve it.*

The amount of proof required in debating is generally less than that required in law. In law, the jury must be convinced beyond a reasonable doubt that the defendant is guilty in order to convict him; in debating, an assertion is established if it is supported by the weight of evidence and logic, even though there still may be room for doubt.

One further distinction is this: In law the jury may disbelieve evidence, even though its accuracy is not disputed. In debating, the judge is measuring the relative skill of the two teams, not deciding the "bedrock merits" of the matter in question. Therefore he is required to accept as valid all arguments backed with reasonable proof (as defined above) until overthrown by the opposing team.

A debate coach once remarked, "The implications here are pretty strong. Does this mean that the judge cannot penalize a team which uses a bare-faced lie as proof? Why not manufacture your evidence?" His point is well taken. Manufactured evidence is so rare in debate as to be almost non-existent, but conceivably it might happen some time. In that event, the following rule would cover the situation:

Rule 5 c. *Facts, presented in a debate as such, must be accurate.*

If the judge is certain that the evidence is deliberately falsified, he is justified in giving the decision to the other team on this point alone. More often, it is simply a matter of interpretation of evidence, and if some error in logic is present, it is up to the other team to find it and point it out.

Rule 5 d. *Any restatement or quotation of an opponent's argument must be accurate.*

A word-for-word quotation, in context, is ideal. This is ordinarily possible when the quotation is short or when one of the members of the team knows shorthand. Under most circumstances, however, the debater finds it necessary to paraphrase his opponent's remarks; for this purpose he needs careful notes and an understanding of his opponent's intent.

Misquotation, whether deliberate or not, unfairly places the other team in a false position and should be studiously avoided.

Rule 5 e. *Visual aids are permissible in debate. Once introduced, they become available for the opponents' use if desired.*

On international questions, one team may desire to point out certain areas on a map. If this be done, the map may also be used by the opposing team. Consequently, it should be left in plain view of the audience, not rolled up and tucked under a table after the first speaker is through with it.

Rule 5 f. *One-sided visual aids must not be exhibited while an opponent is speaking, unless the opponent specifically requests that this be done.*

Some teams prepare an outline of their case on a large poster, and exhibit this poster during the first constructive speech. If this be done, the poster should be removed at the end of the speech so that it does not distract from the attention given the next speaker.

If the next speaker feels that the constructive speech could be refuted more effectively with the poster in front of the audience, he may ask that it be put up again, in which case his request is, of course, granted.

Preferably, visual aids should be introduced in the constructive speeches, rather than held until the rebuttals.

QUESTIONING IN OREGON DEBATE

Several forms of Oregon cross-examination debating are employed in high school and college debates. Unless otherwise specified in the contract, in the league rules, in the tournament rules, or in the pre-debate correspondence, the following rules are presumed to apply:

Rule 6 a. *The questioner may ask any fair, clear question that has a direct bearing on the debate.*

The questioner may use the period (1) to build up any part of his own case, (2) to tear down any part of the opposition's case, or (3) to ascertain facts, such as the opposition's position on a certain issue, that can be used later in the debate.

The questioner is allowed wide latitude with regard to the relevancy of the questions. The chairman has the right to rule questions irrelevant if the irrelevancy is carried to extremes, but this is almost never done in practice. There are two major reasons for this. First, well-thought-out lines of questioning leading to dilemmas, inconsistencies, or impossible positions are considered good debating and are undoubtedly enjoyed by the audience and at least half of the debaters; they can be used to best advantage when the opposition does not realize where the questions are leading. Second, since the time of the questioning period is ordinarily presumed to exist for the benefit of the questioner, the witness has no ground on which to object if the questioner wishes to waste his time on irrelevant questions; the questioner is harming himself and not the opposition.

> **Rule 6 b.** *The questioner controls the time. He may interrupt the witness to request shorter or more direct answers, or to indicate that the answer is sufficient.*

If the witness filibusters, the questioner can always break in with, "Thank you, Mr. Jones, that answers the question. And now . . . ."

> **Rule 6 c.** *The questioner must confine himself to questions and not make statements or comments.*

The appropriate time for comments on the answers given by the witness is the following constructive speech, or the rebuttal period. If the questioner wishes to introduce facts into the questioning, he need not make statements to do so; they can always be phrased as questions in the form, "Are you aware that . . .?" and "Do you agree that . . .?"

> **Rule 6 d.** *The witness must answer every question unless he can show that it would be unfair or unreasonable to expect him to answer.*

In short, he may not decline to answer simply because he prefers not to commit himself; he must have a valid reason. An example of an unfair question would be one that is too detailed or technical, such as, "In your plan for socialized medicine, how will you handle the heart disease problem?" The witness may, if he chooses, point out that this is a technical problem, and that he does not know the answer.

On the other hand, the chairman should not allow the witness to use this excuse to avoid answering legitimate questions. For instance, the chairman should direct the witness to answer the question, "On what basis are you going to determine the number of doctors in any given locality?" This is a reasonable and important question; it cannot be evaded except by the admission that the team does not know what it wants to recommend.

The witness should not be allowed to make the excuse that his partner will cover the point in a later speech. While this may be true enough, one of the objectives of Oregon debate is to allow both teams to obtain such information whenever they desire it; therefore, the chairman should direct the witness to answer. For example, suppose the questioner asked, "Are you going to set up a system of clinics?" The witness should not be allowed to postpone the answer by saying, "My partner will cover the mechanism of our plan in his constructive speech." He is required to answer, but he should welcome the opportunity because it gives him a chance to build up his own case while consuming the time of the questioner. This gives his partner that much more time for other matters in his constructive speech.

Borderline cases will arise, and in general the chairman should support the questioner if it appears that the answers are important to the debate.

Rule 6 e. *The witness may request that the question be repeated or rephrased if it is not clear.*

In this manner, the witness can protect himself against poorly worded questions without appeals to the chair.

Rule 6 f. *The witness must give answers as short and clear as the question warrants. He is not confined to yes-or-no answers.*

Thus, when the question can reasonably be answered in a few words, the witness is obligated to give such a reply. When the questioner inadvertently or deliberately asks a question requiring a lengthy reply (such as "Why?"), the witness has a perfect right to continue with his reply until the question is completely answered or until the questioner interrupts.

Rule 6 g. *The witness must confine himself to answers, and not question the questioner or make comments on other subjects.*

The purpose of this procedure, of course, is to prevent either debater from turning the questioning period into a constructive speech or quibbling match.

Rule 6 h. *Each speaker is questioned as soon as he concludes his constructive speech.*

Until recent years, one version of Oregon debate provided that all the questioning be done between the constructive speeches and the rebuttals. That version seems obsolete today.

Rule 6 i. *The witness must answer the questions put to him without consulting his colleague.*

The purpose of this rule is to prevent unnecessary delays in the questioning period and to enable the debaters to concentrate certain types of questions on certain types of witnesses. A strong team will usually direct its most important questions at the weaker of the opponents.

Rule 6 j. *Either debater may appeal to the chair to enforce the customary questioning procedure. The time consumed in such appeals and their settlement is not counted.*

Appeals to the chair are rare; competent debaters generally find it possible to settle their difficulties without formal protest. It is, however, frequently necessary for the chairman to interrupt inexperienced debaters to remind them that the questioner must confine himself to questions and the witness must confine himself to answers. Later, after the debaters have become accustomed to Oregon style, the problem seldom arises.

Direct Questions in Standard Debate

During the regular constructive speeches of standard (non-Oregon) debates, a direct question or two is sometimes asked with the expectation that it will be answered in the next constructive speech of the opposition. The following rules apply:

Rule 7 a. *During the constructive speeches of non-Oregon debate, the speaker may ask a reasonable number of direct questions for the opposing team to answer in its own speaking period.*

The number of such questions must necessarily be small (say one or two per speech) for otherwise the next speaker could justifiably point out that the number of questions was so large that any attempt to answer them all would consume so much of his speaking time that his regular speech would be sharply curtailed.

Rule 7 b. *At the time the questions are asked, the speaker must make clear that he really desires answers and is not asking rhetorical questions. If he fails to do this, there is no obligation on the part of the opposing team to reply.*

In the majority of cases, the intent of the speaker will be clear from his manner and from the nature of the questions. The rhetorical question is often of the "flag-waving" variety, for instance, "Is America to be chained to the ambitions of unscrupulous foreign dictators? Are we to lose the rights we have fought so hard to preserve?" When the speaker really expects an answer, the question generally refers to the opposing team's position on some major issue. Rhetorical questions, or questions that may be mistaken as such, need not be answered; the judge and audience should simply consider them part of the speech itself.

One worthwhile practice is for the speaker to hand the question in written form to the opposing team as he talks. Then his intent cannot be mistaken, and evasion is difficult.

Rule 7 c. *When the above condition has been met, the opposing team must either answer or show good reason for not answering.*

Preferably, the answer should be given in the next speech.

If the question pertains to minor details or is otherwise unfair (if, for instance, it is of the "Have you stopped stealing from the corner store?" variety), the nature of the question should be pointed out to the judge and audience. If convinced that it is unfair, the judge must ignore the question. If a reasonable inquiry is not answered, however, the judge must presume that the team failing to reply has no reply, and should consider the point settled against the side failing to answer. When the question is of major importance (that is, when it throws doubt on the validity of one of the alleged advantages or disadvantages), failure to reply could conceivably alter the decision. It should be recognized, however, that the most serious effect of such circumstances would be to refute completely one or more of the alleged advantages or disadvantages, and that the judge must not place greater emphasis on such refutation than if it occurred in the normal manner in the speeches and rebuttals.

Refutation and Rebuttal

The rebuttal period is a time for refutation and summary; in fact, such emphasis has been placed on summary that some writers now refer to the "rebuttal-summary" period. Sometimes one team believes that it has completely refuted the other team's arguments before the final speech starts, and then it may be devoted entirely to summary.

In all fairness to the opposing team, the constructive arguments of a team should be established in the constructive speeches, to allow time for the opposition to answer. Consequently, the following rule is well established:

Rule 8 a. *No new constructive arguments may be introduced in the rebuttal period.*

A constructive argument is generally an alleged advantage or disadvantage in one of the proposed plans. All such arguments must be brought out in the constructive speeches.

Constructive arguments introduced in the rebuttal must be disregarded by the judge, with only one exception:

Rule 8 b. *New constructive arguments may be introduced in the rebuttal period if the rebuttal is the first opportunity to answer a direct question and if these new arguments answer the question.*

The long-standing policy against new constructive arguments in the rebuttal period exists to protect teams from the last-minute introduction of new arguments by their opponents. If a team lets down the bars by an indiscreet question, it no longer deserves this protection; accordingly, the opposition may, if it desires, take advantage of the situation by introducing new constructive arguments in rebuttal. Such instances are rare because most teams find it desirable to introduce their constructive arguments early enough in the debate to support them with adequate evidence.

Rule 8 c. *Refutation may take place in any part of the debate and is not limited to the rebuttal period.*

The above rule is so well understood that its mention would be unnecessary were it not that sometimes young debaters claim otherwise. "Refutation" includes the introduction of new evidence, when used to counter a point raised by the opposition.

> **Rule 8 d.** *Either team, when advocating a plan of action, must explain that plan early enough in the debate so that the opposing team has a constructive speech in which to reply.*

Advantages and disadvantages in a proposed plan of action are generally considered new constructive arguments; and new constructive arguments are not permitted in rebuttal (Rule 8 a). Therefore each team must give the other an opportunity to bring out new arguments of this kind before the rebuttals begin.

From the standpoint of the affirmative team, the rule is not particularly important. The affirmative can delay the explanation of its plan until the second constructive speech if it chooses, since the negative still has a constructive speech in which to bring out the defects of the plan before the rebuttals.

From the standpoint of the negative team, however, the rule is significant. Where there are only two constructive speeches per team, the negative must propose any counterplan in its first constructive speech. If the negative waits until the second constructive speech to introduce the counterplan, the affirmative is forced to ignore it or present new constructive arguments in rebuttal.

If the affirmative is on its toes when the negative violates this principle, it can refuse to discuss the matter, pointing out that the negative left it no constructive time in which to bring out the disadvantages. The judge then considers the counterplan irrelevant, out of the debate, and does not consider it in his decision. This, in effect, penalizes the negative.

If, on the other hand, the affirmative chooses to meet the counterplan in the short time remaining, it does so knowing full well that it will be working under a handicap. Therefore, if the affirmative elects this course it is not entitled to any special sympathy; the judge simply reaches his decision on the basis of the arguments presented.

The last affirmative rebuttal presents special problems of its own, since it is the last speech of the debate and the negative has no opportunity for reply. One such problem is covered by this principle:

Rule 8 e. *The affirmative must, if possible, reply to the major negative arguments before the last rebuttal.*

Suppose this rule were not followed. Suppose, for instance, that the affirmative had opportunity to answer some important negative argument earlier in the debate, but failed to do so until the last speech. The negative, having no speech in which to reply, is unfairly handicapped.

If the negative rebuttalist anticipates this problem, he can make the affirmative look very bad by pointing out, as he summarizes, that the affirmative had opportunity to answer this argument earlier, and they did not do so, so any new defense dragged out at the last minute is under suspicion.[5]

Suppose, however, that the negative does not anticipate the problem, and the affirmative does step out of bounds in that final speech. Suppose, for example, that the final speech contains a serious misquotation, or inaccurate facts that seem rather important, or new constructive arguments. What protection does the negative have? What can it do?

There are two methods for preventing unfairness of this kind. Either (1) the judge must be required to recognize and discard such material from the last rebuttal, or (2) some method must be developed to permit the negative to call the attention of the judge and audience to the situation. Since the negative team can recognize inaccurate quotations or facts more easily than the judge, the following rule seems to provide the preferable solution:

Rule 8 f. *If the negative believes that the affirmative is making unfair use of the last rebuttal, it may ask for the floor to point out the situation. The affirmative may then defend the statements in question or correct them and apologize.*

[5] Brooks Quimby, *So You Want to Discuss and Debate*, 2d ed. (Portland, Maine, J. W. Walch, 1954), p. 117-18.

If the judge determines that the negative charges are true, he penalizes the affirmative by throwing out the arguments in question. If he determines that the negative charges are unjustified, no action is necessary. It seems preferable for the judge to state, before the affirmative speaker resumes his remarks, whether the arguments are to be thrown out or not, for only in this way will the affirmative rebuttalist know whether to continue in the same vein.

The judge makes no distinction between the last rebuttal and any other speech unless the negative points out some unfairness.

The time consumed in appeals and their settlement is not counted.

JUDGING

One basic principle underlies debate judging:

Rule 9 a. *The team doing the better debating is the winner.*

Conceivably, more than one process might be employed to determine which team does the better debating. Indeed, since the beginning of intercollegiate debating a number of such methods have been proposed and utilized. Probably the most universally acceptable criterion would be this:

Rule 9 b. *The team doing what the proposition requires is the winner.*

Debate topics are worded so that one team must succeed and one team must fail in meeting the requirements of the proposition. The successful team, having done the better debating, is declared victorious.

When the topic is expressed in the usual form as a proposition of policy, the judge's criterion for determining the winning team may be expressed in this form:

Rule 9 c. *The decision is given to the affirmative if it succeeds in showing that the proposed plan should be* *adopted. The decision is given to the negative if the affirmative fails to show that the proposal should be adopted.*

The judge must remain strictly neutral and impartial with regard to the subject matter for debate. He cannot aid one team or the other by injecting his own personal opinions into the decision. This principle is applied in several ways:

Rule 9 d. *The judge must base his decision entirely on the material presented, without regard for other material which he may happen to possess.*

Arguments or evidence which occur to the judge, but which are not employed in the debate, have no place in the decision. However, if the judge happens to possess some significant facts not employed in the debate, it would be helpful for him to mention them after his decision, as a suggestion for future use.

Rule 9 e. *The judge is required to accept as true all arguments backed by reasonable proof (as defined above) until such arguments are overthrown by the opposing team.*

The judge has no right to consider an argument weak unless the opposing team shows that it is, or unless the team making the argument baldly asserts it and fails to support it with adequate evidence or reasoning.

Rule 9 f. *The judge must not accept ideas which are not backed by reasonable proof.*

Unsupported assertions and purely emotional appeals must not be considered. The use of emotion is legitimate in driving home a point, and is to be encouraged in many instances, but the point must also be supported by evidence or logic if it is to be considered.

Impartiality also applies to the judgment of the debate techniques employed. Harlan [6] puts it this way:

> The danger of using coaches for judges is that they have their own ideas about how best to prove each side, and, regardless of how good your proof might be, if you do not prove it as they would, there will be a tendency to discount your arguments.

Perhaps this does not apply to the majority of coaches who serve as judges. But in those instances where the coach-judge does swerve from impartiality, the criticism is valid. Each team has the right to make use of whatever arguments it desires, and the judge may not penalize a team for failing to make use of an argument or type of case he considers good. The entire decision must be based on what the teams accomplish, not on what the judge personally believes a good debate case on that subject to be.

VIOLATIONS

Rules of debate exist to define the procedure and the playing field. They are similar to rules of football in that violation means a penalty of some sort but not necessarily loss of the game. Of course, in a tight situation the penalty could, in either game, mean the difference between victory and defeat.

Rules of debate are designed so that the teams suffer the natural consequences of their actions. There is no parallel in debate to football's five-yard penalty, but there is a close parallel to an out-of-bounds run in football: If the runner goes out of bounds, the play is stopped at that point; any gain made off the playing field is disallowed. In debate, any gain made outside of the established procedure is disallowed.

Suppose, for example, that a team brings up new constructive arguments in rebuttal. Since there is a rule against it, the judge would be required to disregard such arguments. This means that the offending team has wasted some of its time, which is the natural penalty one would expect. No additional penalty is placed on top of this natural one.

[6] Roy Earle Harlan, *Strategic Debating* (Boston, Chapman and Grimes, 1940) p. 98.

Again, suppose that a team makes assertions without proof. Since there is a rule which says that he who asserts must prove, the judge will decline to accept unsupported assertions. This is the natural penalty for violation of the rule. No additional penalty is inflicted.

This may be summarized as follows:

Rule 10. *Any gains made outside of the established procedure are disallowed.*

2

CUSTOMS AND PROCEDURES

The debating customs presented in this chapter, although generally followed, are after all merely conventions and may be disregarded by the general consent of those concerned.

Tournament Procedure

Tournament debating is rapidly supplanting contract debating throughout the United States. This trend evidently is due to (1) the greater convenience for the debaters themselves, (2) the lessened administrative work for those whose responsibility it is to arrange the debates, and (3) the decreased cost. The tournament is more convenient for the debaters because each team is expected to prepare one subject for the series rather than a new subject for each debate. While the annual national topic has to a large extent eliminated much of the nuisance of preparing many different topics, schools relying on contract debating still find it necessary to use an assortment of subjects.

Another advantage of the tournament is that it decreases the amount of administrative work required. Of course, arranging a tournament requires a great deal of work on the part of the host, but even so the total amount of administrative work throughout the year is lessened for both host and visiting teams. It is easier to accept an invitation to a tournament than to correspond with each of these schools individually. It is easier to secure judges for a given number of debates if these debates are all held at one time than if they are spread over the year. It is easier to arrange lodging, meals, and debating halls for a tournament than for the same number of individual debates. The third and perhaps greatest advantage of the tournament is that it enables schools to take part in a more extensive debating program at no greater cost. The number of debates per mile traveled is higher in tournament debating than in contract debating, even though the former may include long trips. Consequently the traveling costs are reduced. Since during tournaments many debates are held in a short period of time, lodging costs and other operating expenses are reduced. Through the use of coaches as judges, the judging fees are eliminated or greatly reduced. The tournament has proved itself more economical than an equal number of individual debates.[1]

Invitations to tournaments are usually issued by an honor society or by some individual school. The invitation includes the topic and timing, the number of teams to be sent by each school, the number of rounds, whether the tournament is to be an elimination or non-elimination one, whether the teams change sides, whether each school is to provide a judge, whether substitutions are to be permitted, eligibility rules, and provisions for lodging and meals. Those schools desiring to attend pay a fee to the host which covers the cost of running the tournament and lodging for the team members and coach, but which usually does not include meals.

After the arrival of the teams, a meeting is held to welcome the guests and to explain the rules of that particular tournament. There are two major types of meets, the elimination contest and the non-elimination contest.

In the elimination tournament, each school is represented by one team which is prepared to defend either the affirmative or negative side of the subject. Opponents and sides are chosen by lot. Each team debates until defeated; winners debate each other until one winning team is left. This type of meet is especially popular where a large number of teams are entered.

In the non-elimination tournament, each school is represented by two teams, an affirmative and a negative. Opponents are chosen by lot. The tournament continues for a certain specified number of debates. When the number of

[1] For details on debate costs see Paul A. Carmack, "Survey of Forensic Finances," *Speech Activities*, 7:5-7, Spring 1951.

teams entered is small, this is until each affirmative has debated each negative team; if the number of teams is large, the tournament must end at some predetermined number of debates. The winning affirmative team and the winning negative team are determined by their won-lost averages. The winning school is determined by the over-all won-lost average of the teams representing that school.

Tournament debating, as such, has few rules apart from those which apply to all debates. Two customs which have become fairly well established are (1) that each debate shall be open to anyone who desires to hear it, thus permitting scouting, and (2) that no team shall be allowed to substitute one debater for another while the tournament is in progress except in case of sickness or other emergency. This latter custom is designed to prevent a team from bringing in fresh debaters with new cases on the second or third day. This is generally considered unfair because the schools located near the tournament are in a better position to provide substitutes than schools which must travel a considerable distance. However, the matter is not of major importance, so that other schools seldom object if one team asks permission to make a substitution.

A sample set of tournament rules, in the form of an invitation, follows:

University of M. . . . Debating Tournament

Invitation: You are cordially invited to attend a debating tournament to be held at the University of M. . . . on February 8 and 9, 1957. The tournament will be limited to sixteen colleges and universities in this area. If any of the first sixteen schools invited are unable to attend, invitations will be extended to other colleges in the vicinity. For this reason, a prompt reply is requested.

Representation: Each school will be represented by one affirmative and one negative team. Each school will participate in a minimum of four rounds for a total of eight debates. At the conclusion of the first four rounds, the eight schools with the best over-all won-lost averages will participate in three additional rounds to determine the tournament winner. The final rounds will be held on the elimination principle with each school represented by one team per round, either the affirmative or the negative, depending on which side of the topic is drawn for that particular round.

Two-man teams will be used. Each participant must be a registered undergraduate student at the institution he represents, and no person is eligible who has participated in more than four years of intercollegiate debating. Women are eligible. No substitutions for the original four men will be permitted except in case of emergency, although a coach may shift men from the affirmative team to the negative team and vice-versa at any time during the tournament.

Each school must bring, in addition to the four debaters, a coach or adviser who is qualified to judge debates. If such an individual is unable to attend, the school is expected to contribute $20 toward the fee paid to a substitute judge.

Schedule: The organization meeting of the tournament will be held at 8 A.M. on February 8, 1957 in Conner Hall. The train from Centerville arrives at 7:30 A.M., and the campus is a short walk from the railroad station.

The debating schedule is as follows:

Friday, February 8, 1957

8:00	Organization meeting, Conner Hall
9:00-10:00	Round 1
1:00- 2:00	Round 2
4:30- 5:30	Round 3
8:00- 9:00	Round 4

Saturday, February 9, 1957

8:30- 9:30	Qualifying round if necessary
10:30-11:30	Round 1 of the finals
2:00- 3:00	Round 2 of the finals
5:30- 6:30	Round 3 of the finals
7:30	Banquet, Baker Hall

Housing and Meals: A tournament fee of $25 per school will cover all administrative costs of the tournament and will, in addition, cover lodging for five persons for the night of February 8, 1957. Those desiring lodging for the nights of February 7, or February 10, may secure the same at a rate of $3 per person per night by requesting such arrangements at least one week before the tournament. Meals will be available at Baker Hall and at numerous cafes and restaurants in town. Each person is expected to provide his own meals except for the banquet Saturday night, which is included in the tournament fee.

Topic and Timing: The topic for debate will be, "Resolved, that the federal government should outlaw labor activities designed to elect candidates for public office." Oregon 8-5-8 timing will be used.

Other Arrangements: All debates will be open to those who desire to attend. At the conclusion of each debate, the judge will present an oral critique of the contest, announcing his decision and the reasons for it. The judge will then confirm his decision in writing on the judge's ballot form, and turn this ballot in to the tournament administrator in Conner Hall at the earliest possible opportunity. As results are received, the tournament administrator will post the tabulation of results on a special bulletin board in Conner Hall. At the conclusion of the tournament the final tabulated results will be mimeographed and distributed to the participants, five copies to each school unless more are requested. It is believed that this summary can be distributed at the conclusion of the banquet Saturday night.

Debating Schedule: At the Friday organization meeting, each school will be assigned a number by lot. The affirmative team of a school will be designated by that school's number followed by the suffix "a." The suffix "n" will designate the school's negative team.

In the following chart, the capital letters indicate the rooms in which the debates will be held.

The small "c" stands for "coach"; the number following the "c" indicates the school with which the coach is affiliated. The combined number is used in the following table to show which debates each coach will judge.

For example, it can be seen from the following table that the affirmative team of College No. 7 meets, in the second round, the negative team of College No. 10 in room F, with the coach of College No. 16 as judge.

The tournament invitation is not always as complete as this example. Frequently the number of participating teams is not known at the time the invitations are issued, so that the schedule cannot be given in as much detail. In this event, the schedule is posted at the beginning of the tournament.

	Round I	Round II	Round III	Round IV
1a vs.	2n A c7	4n P c10	6n O c13	8n N c16
2a vs.	3n B c8	5n A c11	7n P c14	9n O c1
3a vs.	4n C c9	6n B c12	8n A c15	10n P c2
4a vs.	5n D c10	7n C c13	9n B c16	11n A c3
5a vs.	6n E c11	8n D c14	10n C c1	12n B c4
6a vs.	7n F c12	9n E c15	11n D c2	13n C c5
7a vs.	8n G c13	10n F c16	12n E c3	14n D c6
8a vs.	9n H c14	11n G c1	13n F c4	15n E c7
9a vs.	10n I c15	12n H c2	14n G c5	16n F c8
10a vs.	11n J c16	13n I c3	15n H c6	1n G c9
11a vs.	12n K c1	14n J c4	16n I c7	2n H c10
12a vs.	13n L c2	15n K c5	1n J c8	3n I c11
13a vs.	14n M c3	16n L c6	2n K c9	4n J c12
14a vs.	15n N c4	1n M c7	3n L c10	5n K c13
15a vs.	16n O c5	2n N c8	4n M c11	6n L c14
16a vs.	1n P c6	3n O c9	5n N c12	7n M c15

When the contest rules, as above, provide for judging by neutral coaches or faculty members, some coaches prefer to bring a colleague to handle the judging so that the coach himself is free to hear his teams participate.

The West Point Tournament

The Rose Bowl of intercollegiate debating is the annual National Invitational Debate Tournament at West Point.

Thirty-four teams, representing all parts of the nation, compete. The preceding year's winner is automatically invited.

To insure fair selection of the other thirty-three teams, the nation is divided into eight districts. A committee of outstanding debate teachers in each district determines which schools will be invited. In some instances, district tournaments are held for this purpose. In other cases, the district committee extends invitations to the schools in their districts that hold the best records for the season.

Eight non-elimination "seeding" rounds are held to determine which teams will enter the elimination rounds. Team matchings in the seeding rounds are determined by these rules:

1. No team debates the same team twice.
2. No team debates a team from its own district.
3. Teams debate opposite sides of the question an equal number of times.
4. Teams debate alternate sides from round to round.
5. Teams are matched according to their won-lost records, winners against winners and losers against losers.

The highest sixteen teams enter the elimination rounds. The elimination schedule provides for strong teams to meet weak teams in order that two strong teams may meet in the finals.

The judging is done by visiting coaches, speech teachers from the eastern United States, and professional men, such as lawyers and doctors, who are experienced in debate judging. There are usually three judges for each debate in the seeding rounds, and five to eleven judges for each debate in the elimination rounds. Criteria for assigning judges are as follows:

1. No judge will judge a team from his own district.
2. No judge will judge the same team twice, unless absolutely necessary, and then on the opposite side.

3. When it is necessary to assign one judge instead of three:
    (a) Teams with the best records are given three judges.
    (b) A team may be required to have a single judge only twice.

The tournament lasts three days. Typically, registration takes place on Wednesday afternoon. Four seeding rounds are held on Thursday and the other four on Friday. The four elimination rounds are held on Saturday.

Appropriate trophies and prizes are awarded the winners.

There is plenty of time for relaxation between rounds, and West Point is noted for its hospitality. The schedule of events varies from year to year, of course, but typical features are tours of the Academy, a parade of the cadet corps, a banquet, and perhaps a movie or other diversion.

The West Point Debate Council, consisting of about 450 cadets, sponsors the tournament. A large and competent cadet staff makes this a smooth-running, well organized affair.

THE NFL TOURNAMENT

The annual high school championship tournament is sponsored by the National Forensic League.

NFL members who win first place in their state league contest, or in the NFL district tournament, are eligible for the national contest. Schools which do not belong to NFL are excluded, but this limitation is not too serious; schools with strong programs are likely to belong to NFL.

The tournament lasts four days, Tuesday through Friday, with perhaps sightseeing or some other special event on Saturday.

Four non-elimination rounds are held, during which each team debates twice on the affirmative and twice on the negative. At the end of the four rounds, all teams having won three debates and those having a total of 70 points on the O'Connor rating scale enter a series of elimination debates to determine the winner.

The O'Connor scale is designed to measure the relative strengths of teams in situations, such as tournaments, where several teams compete against each other. It "awards 25 points for each debate won, 10 points for each debate won by an opponent you defeat, and subtracts 10 points for each debate lost by a team to which you lose." As can readily be appreciated, this places a premium on being able to defeat strong opponents.

If more than sixteen teams are eligible to enter the elimination rounds, those with the lowest ratings are matched in a qualifying round to reduce the number to sixteen.

In the elimination rounds, teams change sides each round and are not paired against a previous opponent if avoidable.

At least three judges determine the winner for each round of debate.

CONTRACT PROCEDURE

The scheduling of individual debates through negotiation between schools today is found primarily in the eastern part of the country (although even there it is rapidly losing ground in relation to the tournament), and in radio and television debates. The contract is sometimes oral but usually written. It includes the time and place of debate; the debate topic, including any definitions agreed upon; the side of the subject each team will have; the number of men on each team; and the timing to be used. Preferably mention is also made of some authoritative set of rules of debating, with the statement that those rules are to be followed in the debate being contracted.

When contract negotiations are going on, one team usually selects the subject, giving the other team its choice of sides. This is done in order to insure an even question. Since one team selects the subject and therefore has opportunity to pick an even one, and since the other team has its choice of sides, neither team is justified in claiming that it has been placed at a disadvantage.

Formerly it was customary for the name of the judge to be included in the contract, but present practice in most states leaves the selection of the judge entirely up to the home team.

The contract usually specifies the financial obligations of the teams; otherwise unpleasant situations might easily arise. The visiting team commonly pays its own traveling expenses, while the home team pays all local expenses, including meals and overnight lodging for the visitors. The "guarantee," or fee paid by the home team to the visitors to defray part of the traveling costs, has disappeared except for international debates held in the United States.

Sometimes in contract debating a team fails to debate as planned. If the debate was scheduled as a decision contest, it is only fair that the defaulting team should consider the debate forfeited. If the circumstances were extenuating, or if sufficient notice was given so that no inconvenience resulted, the other team may expressly or by implication waive its right to win by forfeit; otherwise both schools should consider the debate a loss for the defaulting team.

CARING FOR GUESTS

The problem of caring for overnight guests in contract debating can be rather serious, particularly where the program is entirely student-run with little or no faculty guidance. Visitors are entitled to every courtesy, and students are sometimes a little inept at this.

In a well-run program, the visitors are told in pre-debate correspondence where to report when they arrive on the campus. A nice gesture is to send them a map of the campus to help them find their way. A typical sequence of events might be something like this:

5:00 P.M. The visitors arrive at the office of the debate director. The director and one or more students from the host school may be there waiting. After a get-acquainted chat, someone escorts the visitors to a dormitory, where they will stay. He asks whether dinner at 6:30 will be all right, and on being told that it will be, he leaves, giving the visitors time to rest.

6:30 P.M. Two students, acting as hosts, knock on the door. They take the visitors to dinner and show them the campus.

7:30 P.M.   The visitors and hosts arrive at the Student Union Building. The opposing debaters meet each other, as well as the chairman, timekeeper, and judge.

The visitors are shown to their table and left alone for last-minute preparations.

If the visiting coach is present, the two coaches sit together.

8:00 P.M.   The debate begins.

9:30 P.M.   The debate over, the whole group adjourns for light refreshments and a social get-together. The evening is enhanced if two or three coeds join the party.

10:30 or   The guests are escorted back to their dorm room. The
11:00 P.M.   hosts inquire about plans for the following morning, and unless a very early start is indicated, they leave meal tickets with the visitors for breakfast.

STAGE FURNISHINGS

The details of the stage equipment, location of the judge, location of the rostrum, method of keeping time, size of the audience, and similar items are handled by the home team. On any item where there is likely to be an important difference of opinion, it is courteous for the home team to ask the visitors their preference, but since arrangements are made well ahead of time, this can seldom be done. Particularly in the case of radio and television debates is it important for the home team to be given complete freedom in the handling of these small details.

Usually the rostrum is in the center of the platform. To the sides, and even with or slightly behind the rostrum, are two small tables facing the audience, one for each team. In Oregon style debates, they are turned at 45° angles, so that the seated debaters half face the speaker; this arrangement makes it possible for the questioner to stand at the rostrum and question the witness at his table. For diagrams of standard and Oregon seating arrangements see pages 48 and 49.

The affirmative sits on the speaker's right, the negative on the speaker's left. The chairman and timekeeper usually sit together in the first row of the audience. The judge sits anywhere in the audience, sometimes near a table so that he can take notes more conveniently. When a table is not available, the judge should be provided with a clip-board on which to write.

The placing of a pitcher of ice water and glasses on each team's table before the debate is an unessential but pleasant custom worth following when possible.

SPEAKING ARRANGEMENTS

The length of the speeches and the speaking arrangement depend on the rules of the tournament or on the contract between the two teams. The following systems are in common use today:

Standard 10-5 timing:

First affirmative constructive speech .... 10 min.
First negative constructive speech 10
Second affirmative constructive speech 10
Second negative constructive speech 10

First negative rebuttal, by first negative speaker ... 5
First affirmative rebuttal, by first affirmative speaker 5
Second negative rebuttal, by second negative speaker 5
Second affirmative rebuttal, by second affirmative
    speaker 5
                                                    ──
                                                    60 min.

This arrangement is probably used more often than any other, in both high school and college debating. Where no speaking order is specified, this arrangement is generally intended. It is thoroughly sound in every respect.

Oregon 8-5-8 timing:

First affirmative constructive speech .... 8 min.
    First affirmative questioned by second negative 5
First negative constructive speech 8
    First negative questioned by first affirmative ... 5
Second affirmative constructive speech 8
    Second affirmative questioned by first negative .. 5

Second negative constructive speech	8
Second negative questioned by second affirmative	5
Negative rebuttal-summary, by first negative speaker	8
Affirmative rebuttal-summary, by first affirmative speaker	8
	—
	68 min.

This is a lively and exciting form of debate. The rapid cross-fire produces a contest with considerable audience appeal. It is used in several high school state leagues and in certain college circles.

Oregon 8-3-4-4 timing:

First affirmative constructive speech	8 min.
First affirmative questioned by second negative ..	3
First negative constructive speech	8
First negative questioned by first affirmative ...	3
Second affirmative constructive speech	8
Second affirmative questioned by first negative ..	3
Second negative constructive speech	8
Second negative questioned by second affirmative	3
Negative rebuttal, by first negative speaker	4
Affirmative rebuttal, by first affirmative speaker	4
Negative rebuttal, by second negative speaker	4
Affirmative rebuttal, by second affirmative speaker ..	4
	—
	60 min.

This plan, used by the National Forensic League for its national high school tournament, is similar to 8-5-8 except that there are two rebuttals per team instead of one. The extra rebuttals are useful in giving each debater an equal amount of speaking time, and in providing another opportunity for refutation.

Some localities follow the practice of having a short intermission between the constructive speeches and the rebuttals in order to give time for the preparation of the concluding speeches. Apparently this practice developed when two-hour debates were common and the intermission was needed by the audience as well as the debaters; the custom has never disappeared, even though most debates today are closer to one hour than two hours in length. Since ordinarily the rebuttalist—if he is a good debater—has plenty of time during the course of the debate to prepare his rebuttal, and since this intermission tends to lessen audience interest in the course of a short debate, the practice is of doubtful value.

The first speaker is occasionally allowed time to express pleasure at meeting the opposing team. In such cases, this time is not included in the time consumed by the debater unless the privilege is abused; certainly the speaker cannot be allowed to ramble on for several minutes telling jokes and getting the audience on his side without including this time in that allotted for his constructive speech. However, it is generally considered more desirable to postpone such remarks until after the decision in order to preserve the competitive spirit of the contest. For this reason, and in order to encourage the speaker to be brief if he does desire to make such remarks, timing begins with the first words of the speaker unless specified to the contrary in the tournament rules or in the contract.

TIMEKEEPING

Several systems of keeping time are in use; timing cards are one of the best. The timekeeper, sitting in the audience near the speakers, holds in his lap a set of cards which indicate to the speaker the number of minutes he has left. The ordinary set consists of twelve cards, numbered from one to ten, together with one marked "½" and one marked "Stop." The cards are of postcard size or larger, and the numbers are large and black so that near-sighted debaters can read them easily. The timekeeper exposes the first ten cards at one-minute intervals, telling the speaker exactly how much time he has left.

When the "Stop" card is reached, the timekeeper indicates not only to the debater, but also to the judge and audience, that any further remarks by the speaker are being made on time to which he is not entitled. This can be done

SEATING ARRANGEMENT, STANDARD TIMING:

AFFIRMATIVE   ROSTRUM   NEGATIVE

CHAIRMAN   TIMEKEEPER

AUDIENCE

SEATING ARRANGEMENT, OREGON TIMING:

NEGATIVE

ROSTRUM

TIMEKEEPER

CHAIRMAN

AUDIENCE

AFFIRMATIVE

by ringing a bell at the end of the scheduled time or by standing until the speaker stops. Under this system, each debater has adequate information at all times regarding the amount of time left, so that there is little or no excuse for speaking overtime.

In radio or television debates, the same system can be used. Here timing cards have the added advantage of being completely silent. If one speaker fails to use all of his allotted time, the unused time can be added to the next speech of that team, thus making sure that the debate will not end too soon. The questioning period is an especially good time to bring the debate back onto schedule in radio debates.

A bell should never be used for any purpose except to indicate that time is up. The bell distracts the audience, drawing attention away from the speaker.

Recently some schools have installed large stop clocks as substitutes for timing cards. These clocks can be set by the timekeeper for any desired length of speech; they indicate at all times the number of minutes and seconds the speaker has left. A bell rings at the end of the scheduled time, but the bell can be disconnected when the clock is used in radio or television debates. If care is used in the selection of the instrument, so that the numbers are large enough to be read easily, and so that the clock indicates the number of minutes remaining rather than the number of minutes which have elapsed, this device is as satisfactory in every respect as the set of timing cards, and has the added advantage of reducing the likelihood of human error.

Clocks currently available for this purpose are:

Gralab Universal Timer, Model 172. $24.95.

Dimco-Gray Company, 207 East Sixth Street, Dayton 2, Ohio. Sold through photographic supply houses.

This is one of the best clocks currently available for the timing of debates. It has a large 8-inch dial, with a total range of 15 minutes. The number of minutes and seconds remaining can be read by the speaker from a considerable distance. A buzzer sounds

at the end of the predetermined period, if desired. The clock can
be stopped for time-outs. An electrical outlet on the side of the
clock can be connected with lights if desired. Black and alumi-
num color scheme. Electric.

Secron Precision Interval Timer, Model 46340. $9.50.

Standard Scientific Supply Corporation, 34 West Fourth
Street, New York 12.

This clock has a 60-minute dial. The small hand indicates the
number of minutes remaining, while the large sweep hand marks
the seconds. The clock can be stopped for time-outs. There is no
buzzer. The minute graduations are rather fine to be read at a
glance, especially if the clock is very far away. However, it
could be used by the timekeeper, or by the speaker if placed on
the rostrum. 4 by 4½ inches. Spring wound.

PRESENTING THE CASE

The Affirmative Case

The first affirmative speaker, in past years, was often expected to:

1. Begin with, "Mr. Chairman, honorable judges, worthy opponents, ladies and gentlemen."
2. Welcome the opposing team.
3. Explain the importance of the debate topic.
4. Explain the origin and history of the problem.
5. Explain the reasons for debating the topic at this time.
6. Define formally each of the terms of the proposition.

Then, if he had any time left, he was permitted to begin the debate. It might be added that in those days debates were more often two hours than one hour in length.

Today, the first affirmative's approach may look more like this:

1. Begin with, "Ladies and gentlemen."
2. Explain the plan his team is recommending.
3. Explain the benefits to be expected from it.

The phrase, "Ladies and gentlemen," should be sufficient to include everyone present. As one judge remarked, "If it doesn't include me, I don't want to be reminded about it." In some circles the first speaker on each side still has a few words of greeting for the opposing team, but remarks of this kind are always short. Debaters are no longer expected to waste valuable speaking time explaining the importance of the debate topic, the origin and history of the problem, and the reasons for debating it at this time.

Formal definitions are sometimes needed, sometimes not. They do have the merit of marking off the playing field. And the teams do need to study the wording very carefully before the debate, in order to make sure that the affirmative's proposed plan of action lies within the framework of the topic. On the other hand, it is not always necessary to spend speaking time during the debate defining "federal government," when everyone present knows exactly what is meant. Instead, the first affirmative explains briefly the plan his team is proposing.

Explaining the plan of action need not take long—a minute or two will do—but it can contribute a great deal to the effectiveness of the presentation. It brings the debate quickly to earth and enables all concerned to follow the significance of the speaker's next remarks.

The broad outline of the plan is sufficient; in most cases, details need not be presented. It is wise, however, to have the details worked out and agreed upon beforehand, to avoid trouble spots and to have the answers ready if needed.

Next, the first affirmative speaker may explain the benefits to be expected from his plan. Perhaps there are three or four. He tells what they are, then shows the importance of each and how his plan will bring it about.

Each advantage should, of course, be backed up by factual evidence. Weak arguments should be left out entirely. Some say that weak arguments should be sandwiched in the middle, between strong ones. This is a mistake, as the debater will quickly discover if he tries it. The only place for a weak argument is in the waste basket.

Finally, the first affirmative speaker should summarize his team's case by listing the benefits.

What does this leave for the second affirmative speaker to do? Should some of the advantages be saved for the second speaker to present? The wisdom of this can be argued either way. It is, however, very effective to leave the second affirmative free to refute the negative case, and to rebuild his own team's advantages. In this way, the affirmative tries to stay one jump ahead of the negative all through the debate.

The Negative Case

There are two [1] possible negative cases: (1) defense of the *status quo,* and (2) support of a counterplan.

The term *"status quo"* means conditions as they are now, with perhaps some minor modifications, such as better administration of existing laws and institutions.

If the negative decides to defend the *status quo,* the affirmative has the burden of proof. It must show that its plan would make things better than they are now.

The term "counterplan" means a whole new course of action, preferably involving some change of principle. To be effective, the counterplan must be something the affirmative cannot recommend under the wording of the topic.

If the negative decides to recommend a counterplan, it assumes the burden of proof for its plan. In effect the negative says, "We agree that things are not so good now, but we think we have a plan that will be better than yours." The negative must show that its plan is better than the affirmative plan.

Effective Case Organization

If the debater wants to win, he should organize his case in a form that the judge and audience can easily follow; this is the consideration of the advantages or disadvantages one at a time. Each advantage or benefit is covered completely before the next is presented. Everyone understands what a benefit or advantage is, so it is easy to see the significance of the speaker's remarks.

For example, when a boy asks a girl to go to the movies, a rational discussion might sound something like this:

> *He:* Let's go to the movies. There's a swell show on at the Bijou that we'll both like.
>
> *She:* But won't it be hot? They don't have air conditioning.

---

[1] Some debate texts maintain that there are four possibilities: (1) defense of the *status quo,* (2) defense of the *status quo* with repairs, (3) straight refutation or denial, and (4) support of a counterplan. The debater will find that in actual practice, these quickly boil down to just two possibilities. (1) and (2) are, for all practical purposes, identical because in either case the affirmative retains the burden of proof. (1) and (3) are identical, because the effect of rejecting any plan of action is to leave things as they are now. So the negative has its choice: Defense of the *status quo* (perhaps with repairs), or support of a counter-plan.

In those few short sentences, both an advantage and a disadvantage were brought out. When a debate case is organized in this manner, it looks something like this:

Status Quo Debate

Affirmative case:

   I. First benefit (of plan over present conditions)
     A. Importance
     B. How it will be attained
  II. Second benefit
     A. Importance
     B. How it will be attained
 III. Third benefit
     A. Importance
     B. How it will be attained

Negative case:

   I. First disadvantage
     A. Importance
     B. How it will come about
  II. Second disadvantage
     A. Importance
     B. How it will come about
 III. Third disadvantage
     A. Importance
     B. How it will come about

That is all there is to it! Is it any wonder that the teams which developed this type of case organization maintained an enviable record over a period of years?

Judges are human. So are the people in the audience, and the other debaters. They all prefer arguments that are clear and easy to follow. Why not keep the outline simple?

Sometimes the negative presents a counterplan. Our movie example might sound something like this:

    He: Let's go to the movies. There's a swell show on at the Bijou that we'll both like.

    She: Oh, Jim, why don't we go swimming instead? It's cooler on a night like this.

Those few sentences brought out an affirmative plan with an advantage, and a counterplan with an advantage.

Here's what the corresponding debate outline looks like:

Counterplan Debate

Negative case:

    I. First benefit (of counterplan over affirmative plan)
        A. Importance
        B. How it will be attained
    II. Second benefit
        A. Importance
        B. How it will be attained
    III. Third benefit
        A. Importance
        B. How it will be attained

Affirmative case:

    I. First disadvantage (of counterplan with respect to affirmative plan)
        A. Importance
        B. How it will come about
    II. Second disadvantage
        A. Importance
        B. How it will come about
    III. Third disadvantage
        A. Importance
        B. How it will come about

INEFFECTIVE CASE ORGANIZATION

When intercollegiate debating was introduced to the United States some seventy-five years ago,[2] many ideas were borrowed from other fields and thrust upon debaters. Some, such as cross-examination procedure, were useful; others, such as the brief, were not. Too often these borrowed procedures led the debater away from, rather than toward, the subject matter on which debates are decided. For many years the more competent coaches have picked the useful

[2] The first known intercollegiate debate in this country took place between Illinois College and Knox College on May 5, 1881, according to David Potter in *Argumentation and Debate* (New York, Dryden Press, 1954), p. 12-13. This was followed one day later by a debate between Rutgers and New York University.

forms and have discarded the rest, but only recently have authors begun to recognize this trend.

One such outmoded form is the syllogism, borrowed from courses in logic. The syllogism seldom finds a place in the modern debate outline or in the speeches themselves. The arguments of the contestants can be reduced to syllogistic form, but the debaters themselves have no incentive for doing so; arguments can be presented and refuted in a much more direct manner than by reduction to syllogisms, which is certain to start technical arguments regarding construction.

Another outmoded form is the brief, borrowed from the law courts, recommended by the early textbook writers for debating use, and now discarded by debate coaches everywhere as more of a hindrance than a help in actual competition. The brief is a formal outline of the argument, containing not only the argument itself but also information on the origin and history of the problem and similar topics that are not always relevant to the debate itself. If the debater attempted to follow such a brief in his speech, he would find all his time consumed before he established any advantages or disadvantages in the proposed plans. Nichols and Baccus [3] state:

> Extempore debating consigned the brief to oblivion. . . . The brief has remained in debate parlance because no one, so far, has had the courage to show it the door.

Why has the brief proved unsuccessful? Simply because it confines the debater to a set of arguments that may be irrelevant from the start and that are almost always irrelevant when the opposition's case is presented. The debater will find it wise to avoid the formal brief altogether, and to use a simple outline of the plan's advantages and disadvantages.

From the brief, the following traditional outline developed:

I. Plan is necessary
II. Plan is practicable

[3] E. R. Nichols and J. H. Baccus, *Modern Debating* (New York, W. W. Norton and Company, 1936), p. 139.

Expressed in other terms, this becomes:

I. There is a need for the federal government to adopt such a program because of evils.
II. The plan will be practicable and desirable.

Surely no one seriously believes that when a boy and girl are discussing whether to go to the movies, the conversation sounds like this:

He: There is a need for a change.
She: But is it practicable and desirable?

The above organization is entirely too vague and fuzzy to stand up against the more specific cases of competent opponents. A better, but still poor, type of organization is:

I. Need for change
   A. Need for first benefit
   B. Need for second benefit
   C. Need for third benefit
II. Mechanism of plan for meeting need
   A. How first benefit will be attained
   B. How second benefit will be attained
   C. How third benefit will be attained

That organization gets down to brass tacks and considers the real issues involved, but fails to tie in the "need" with the proposed plan of action. Each benefit is considered twice, once in relation to the need for that particular advantage, and once in relation to the mechanism for bringing it about. The net result is that debaters present less "need" than certain of their proposals demand; in the same debate they show that certain situations are bad but fail to show how their plan would correct these particular situations. Furthermore, since each advantage is considered in two places rather than in one place, the judge and audience can easily become confused as to just what has been proved.

EVIDENCE

The purpose of evidence is to support the claimed benefits or disadvantages.

Evidence, to be effective, should be pertinent and factual. It may consist of statistics, trends, or examples. While the debater may find the evidence he needs in literature on the subject, the chances are that at some point along the line he will have to ask himself, "Just what evidence would be helpful in proving this benefit?" Knowing what he is looking for, perhaps he can find it. Background reading is helpful early in the season in getting the feel of the topic, but research for specific facts or cases is almost always necessary before the team can feel prepared.

A card file is convenient for recording the volume and page number for each bit of evidence uncovered.

It is not necessary, in the actual debate, for the speaker to give the source of every fact brought out. He could probably make the statement, "At the time of the last census, there were sixty-two million people living in urban areas of 25,000 or more," without fear of contradiction. The statement, however, is stronger if he adds, "according to the latest edition of the *United States Statistical Abstract*."

If challenged, the debater should be prepared to give the volume and page number for every fact he uses. It can be very embarrassing to him if he does not have this information at his fingertips.

Some debaters like to quote opinions. Opinions are not worth much, except possibly for admissions "against interest." The principal purpose in collecting opinions is to have them ready if needed for refutation. When the opposition quotes an opinion or two, the debater can point out that opinions are easy to quote, and quote one or two himself on the opposite side. He can then point out that the topic is being debated because of this difference of opinion. He may even rub salt in the wound, if he can do so with a twinkle in his eye, by asking the opposition to come forward for the rest of the debate and meet the issues with facts.

Sources of evidence are almost unlimited. The encyclopedias, almanacs, and government reports provide basic factual data. Debate handbooks are valuable, particularly in leading to other sources. Opinion magazines sometimes suggest arguments and factual material that otherwise might be overlooked. Some of the leading publications of especial interest to debaters are listed in the bibliography of this book.

A Suggested Time Schedule

In a debate where the negative offers a straight negative *status quo* case, each speaker should attempt to contrast the affirmative proposal with present conditions. The time schedule might look something like this:

First Affirmative:

1. Explain plan briefly .... 1.0 min.
2. a. List advantages of plan over *status quo* 0.5
   b. Discuss each 8.0
   c. Summarize by again listing 0.5

                                                    10.0 min.

First Negative:

1. a. List objections to affirmative plan (in the form of defects or disadvantages) .... 0.5 min.
   b. Discuss each 5.0
   c. Summarize by again listing 0.5
2. Refute the claimed advantages of the affirmative plan, discussing the strongest points first 3.5
3. Summarize by again listing the disadvantages of the affirmative plan 0.5

                                                    10.0 min.

Second Affirmative:

1. a. Reiterate the benefits to be accrued from the affirmative plan by listing them .... 0.5 min.
   b. Rebuild where necessary 5.0
   c. Again list 0.5
2. Refute the claimed disadvantages of the proposal 3.5
3. Summarize by again listing the benefits the plan will bring about 0.5

                                                    10.0 min.

Second Negative:

   1. a. Reiterate objections to the affirmative pro-
         posal by listing them .... 0.5 min.
     b. Rebuild where necessary 5.0
     c. Again list 0.5
   2. Refute the claimed advantages of the proposal .. 3.5
   3. Summarize by again listing the defects of the
     plan 0.5

                                           10.0 min.

Negative Rebuttal:

   1. a. List the defects of the affirmative proposal .. 0.5 min.
     b. Discuss these in the summary, pointing out
         how the affirmative attacked these points and
         how each attack was answered. If any major
         attacks were left unrefuted by the preceding
         negative speaker, fill in the gaps 2.0
     c. Summarize by again listing the disadvantages
         of the affirmative plan 0.5
   2. Discuss the alleged advantages of the affirma-
     tive plan and point out how each of these points
     was refuted by the negative 1.5
   3. Conclude by again listing the disadvantages of
     the affirmative plan 0.5

                                           5.0 min.

Affirmative Rebuttal:

   1. a. List the advantages of the affirmative plan
         over the *status quo* .... 0.5 min.
     b. Discuss these in summary, pointing out how
         the negative attacked these points and how
         each attack was answered. Reply to any
         major attacks not already refuted 2.0
     c. Summarize by again listing the benefits to be
         derived from the proposal 0.5
   2. Discuss the claimed defects in the plan, showing
     how each of these points was refuted by the
     affirmative. Make such refutation where necessary 1.5
   3. Conclude by again listing the advantages of the
     plan over the *status quo* 0.5

                                           5.0 min.

In a debate where the negative offers a counterplan, each speaker should attempt to contrast the two plans. The time schedule may work out like this:

First Affirmative:

1. Explain plan briefly .... 1.0 min.
2. a. List advantages of plan over *status quo* 0.5
   b. Discuss each 8.0
   c. Summarize by again listing 0.5

                                            ——
                                            10.0 min.

First Negative:

1. Propose counterplan and explain briefly .... 1.0 min.
2. a. List the ways in which the counterplan is
      superior to the affirmative proposal 0.5
   b. Discuss each 8.0
   c. Summarize by again listing 0.5

                                            ——
                                            10.0 min.

Second Affirmative:

1. a. List the advantages of affirmative plan over
      negative counterplan, using the same list the
      first affirmative speaker used if possible ..... 0.5 min.
   b. Discuss each 5.0
   c. Summarize by again listing 0.5
2. Refute the claimed advantages of the counterplan over the affirmative plan, discussing the
   strongest points first 3.5
3. Summarize by again listing the advantages of
   the affirmative plan over the counterplan 0.5

                                            ——
                                            10.0 min.

Second Negative:

1. a. List the advantages of the counterplan over
      the affirmative proposal .... 0.5 min.
   b. Rebuild these points where necessary 5.0
   c. Summarize by again listing 0.5
2. Refute the claimed advantages of the affirmative plan over the counterplan, discussing the
   strongest ones first 3.5
3. Summarize by again listing the advantages of
   the counterplan over the affirmative plan 0.5

                                            ——
                                            10.0 min.

Negative Rebuttal:

1. a. List the advantages of counterplan over
      affirmative plan .... 0.5 min.
   b. Discuss these in summary, pointing out how
      the affirmative attacked these points and how
      each attack was answered. If any major
      attacks were left unrefuted by the preceding
      negative speaker, fill the gaps 2.0
   c. Summarize by again listing the advantages of
      the counterplan over the affirmative proposal 0.5
2. Discuss the alleged advantages of the affirmative
   plan over the counterplan and point out how each
   of these points was refuted by the negative 1.5
3. Conclude by again listing the advantages of the
   counterplan over the affirmative plan 0.5
                                                      ———
                                                 5.0 min.

Affirmative Rebuttal:

1. a. List the advantages of the affirmative proposal
      over the counterplan .... 0.5 min.
   b. Discuss these in summary, pointing out how
      the negative attacked these points and how
      each attack was answered. Reply to any
      major attacks not already refuted 2.0
   c. Summarize by again listing the advantages of
      the affirmative proposal over the counterplan 0.5
2. Discuss the alleged advantages of the counterplan
   over the affirmative plan and point out how each
   of these points was refuted by the affirmative.
   Make such refutation where necessary 1.5
3. Conclude by again listing the advantages of the
   affirmative plan over the counterplan 0.5
                                                      ———
                                                 5.0 min.

USE OF NOTES

The debater is entitled to carry an outline of the case
with him to the rostrum when he speaks. Much as coaches
hate the excessive use of notes, the debater must have (1)
a short outline of the case, probably in the form of double-
summary sheets, and (2) cards with any figures or quotations that he intends to use. Lahman [4] says,

[4] Carroll P. Lahman, *Debate Coaching* (New York, H. W. Wilson Company, 1936), p. 104.

While we are considering outlines, a word should be said concerning the outline that is used to speak from in the practice or actual debate. It is probably safe to say that it is only the exceptional debater, even in college, who can be trusted to speak with absolutely no notes. On the other hand . . . speaking notes should be reduced to a minimum. Under no circumstances should the manuscript of a speech be tolerated.

Notes are an evil that must be permitted in certain circumstances, but the use of a written speech is never necessary; it seriously weakens the speaker's delivery and therefore destroys much of his effectiveness.

Effective Summary

It is not enough for the debater to build and organize his case properly; he must present it so clearly that everyone, including the judge, understands his line of argument. There is an easy way of accomplishing this. It is so simple that many debaters are inclined to label the method "obvious" and then promptly forget to make use of it. The method is simply the repetition of the claimed advantages and disadvantages so often that no one could possibly forget them. In every speech, without exception, the debater should list, at least twice, all of the benefits or defects asserted by his team. This should be done whether he intends to discuss each point himself or not, because only through constant repetition by all of the debaters on the team can the points be driven home. He should list each point by number, "Benefit Number One" or "Defect Number Three," thus keeping the outline of the case clear in the mind of judge and audience.

This procedure is admittedly simple; its very simplicity makes it effective in presenting the case and thus in winning debates. The first affirmative speaker, in most instances, should open his speech something like this:

Ladies and gentlemen, my colleague and I are proposing this evening that the federal government, through constitutional amendment, abolish the closed shop, union shop, and other forms of union maintenance-of-membership that force workers to belong to unions against their will. We maintain that our plan will result in three major benefits, namely,

1. . . .
2. . . .
3. . . .

We will discuss each of these benefits in turn, showing how sorely each is needed and how our plan will bring each one about.

During the debater's discussion of the alleged advantages or disadvantages, he should always refer to his own team's points by number. At the conclusion of each speech he should summarize, again listing by number all of the benefits or defects claimed by his team. This should be done in every constructive speech and in every rebuttal speech.

Consistent use of this device brings surprisingly good results not only because frequent listing of the points drives them home to the judge and audience, but also because it forces the debaters to have their material clearly organized, and to understand that organization. This is one of the most effective methods yet discovered for presenting cases clearly.

Harlan [5] clearly pointed out the importance of summary when he wrote:

> Three old and mighty good rules are: (1) Tell them what you are going to tell them. (2) Tell them. (3) Tell them what you have told them. . . . Years of experience lead us to say that no debate should close without a summary. . . . A summary can be made so powerful in that last negative rebuttal that, unless the last affirmative speaker is extra powerful, he never gets into the debate at all, for it is closed in the mind of the judge. On the other hand, the last affirmative summary can be made so strong that it will win, regardless of what the negative may have previously said in the debate. . . . Whatever you do, don't expect the poor judge to remember everything that is said in the course of a debate. . . . So be sure and "tell them what you have told them."

This advice is applicable not only to the rebuttal but to the constructive speeches as well.

[5] R. E. Harlan, *Strategic Debating* (Boston, Chapman and Grimes, 1940), p. 152, 153.

4

CROSS-EXAMINATION

In an Oregon style debate each questioning period can be a stimulating mental battle or it can be a garden variety quibbling match, depending on the technique of the participants, particularly the questioner.

The first, and hardest, thing inexperienced debaters have to learn about cross-examination debate is that the questioner is supposed to stick to questions, and the witness to answers. There is such a temptation to talk back!

Practice is the answer. During the first two or three Oregon debates, an alert chairman will be needed to break in to remind the questioner to stick to questions, and to remind the witness to stick to answers. Debaters quickly get the idea, and from that point on, the fun begins.

The questioning periods of an ordinary Oregon debate require at least as much preparation as the constructive and rebuttal speeches, if not more. One does not become an effective questioner or an astute witness overnight; planning and practice are both needed in abundance, as well as better-than-average intelligence. One cannot do much about his intelligence, but there is no limit to the planning and practicing he can do.

The questioner must know definitely where he is going and how he intends to get there. Vague lines of questioning are certain to fail. A long-standing rule-of-thumb used by lawyers in cross-examination is, "Don't ask a question if you don't know the answer." This is generally applicable in debate, the major exception being when the questioner desires to determine the witness's plan of action or position on a certain issue. For the most part, the skillful questioner leads the witness along by asking questions that permit only one answer, or that are favorable to the cause of the questioner, no matter how answered.

The witness, in turn, must be careful about giving unqualified "yes" or "no" answers. He can be certain that the questioner is out after his scalp, no matter how friendly the examiner's tone of voice may be. Unqualified answers are particularly vulnerable to attack, and although the witness may think at the end of the questioning period that no harm has been done by his unequivocal answers, those statements may be quoted by the opposition later in the debate with telling effect.

On the other hand, many debaters inexperienced in Oregon style tend to be too timid; afraid to make definite statements of policy, they hedge on every question. This naturally leaves the impression in the mind of judge and audience that the witness's case must be very weak, or he would not mind discussing the problem in a frank manner.

DETERMINING THE OTHER TEAM'S POSITION

Questioning is an especially good opportunity to find out the other team's position on certain issues. Sometimes the affirmative is rather vague about what it is recommending. If this information is important to the negative in order that it may establish a counterplan, the negative questioner may spend some time determining these details.

Or, the negative may be the vague team. They may talk about possible alternatives without saying whether they are recommending the *status quo* or one of the alternatives. The affirmative, in this case, would probably ask them point-blank, at the first opportunity, just what they do favor.

PILING UP EVIDENCE

Another good use of the questioning period is to pile up evidence. A whole series can be devoted to one point, with item after item of evidence introduced to support it. The

technique is to ask the witness if he "is aware" of each item
of evidence.

Here is how it works:

Q. Have you ever visited Washington, D.C.?

A. Yes, I have. Several times.

Q. You probably know, then, that railroad passengers arrive at
Union Station? And that airline passengers arrive at National Airport?

A. Yes, that's right.

Q. Are these two terminals in competition with each other?

A. I should say they are!

Q. That is, Union Station serves the railroad industry in the
same way that National Airport serves the airline industry?

A. Yes, that's quite accurate.

Q. And Union Station is owned and operated by the railroads?

A. Yes, it is.

Q. While National Airport is owned and operated by the government?

A. Right.

Q. And is that situation typical of other cities?

A. Yes. Some cities have more than one railroad station or more
than one airport. But railroad stations are owned and operated by the railroads, while airports are owned and operated
by some governmental agency.

Q. Is that generally true?

A. Yes. I don't know of even one exception.

Q. We seem to be getting along quite well. No controversy at
all on the basic facts, at least so far, is there?

A. No.

Q. All right, now let's consider the financial aspects of that situation. Construction costs are a pretty big item, so let's take
a look at them. Did the railroads pay for the construction of
Union Station?

A. I assume they did. At least, that's typical.

Q. And if any improvements are made from time to time, are
they paid for by the railroads?

A. Surely.

Q. Did you know that after all these years, it still costs the railroads $1000 per *day* in interest on this money?

A. No, I didn't.

Q. While National Airport was built at taxpayers' expense, to
the tune of some $28 million?

A. Yes.

Q. Is that fair to the railroads or to the public?

A. Well . . .

Q. Before you answer, maybe you'd like to consider some other aspects. Operating costs, for example. Is it true that the railroads pay all of the operating costs of Union Station?

A. Yes, but the airlines do the same thing. They pay the operating costs of National Airport.

Q. All right. Let's examine the facts and see if they do. Did you know that for the year ending June 30, 1954, the airlines paid $354,000 toward the operating costs of National Airport?

A. I'll accept your figure.

Q. Did you know that there was a net deficit of $658,000, paid by the taxpayers?

A. I haven't seen the official financial statement.

Q. Would you care to look over the copy I have here in my hand, before your next speech?

A. I'll accept your figures.

Q. So the airlines paid only one-third as much as they should have, toward the operating costs of National Airport?

A. That's what the figures seem to indicate.

Q. Is it fair to make the railroads pay their own operating expenses, while the government picks up the check for two-thirds of the airlines' share?

A. Well . . .

Q. Is it fair to the taxpayers? That is, you and me?

A. No, I guess it couldn't be called fair. But there are other arguments.

Q. All right, so we have some area of agreement. Now let's consider taxes. Did you know that Union Station pays $2000 per *day* in taxes?

A. I don't question the figure.

Q. While National Airport, government owned, is tax-exempt?

A. Yes.

Q. Is that fair to the railroads or to the taxpayers?

A. (Silence)

Q. Thank you. No more questions.

If the evidence is strong enough—as it should be if this method of questioning is used—it is sometimes possible to ask the witness to agree with the conclusion, as in the above illustration. The conclusion, usually, is a benefit or disadvantage in one of the plans.

There is the danger, of course, that the witness will disagree with the conclusion. He is almost duty-bound to disagree. However, if the questioner does his job, he will be on such solid ground that the witness will have to agree or appear to be a dunce.

Establishing An Advantage Or Disadvantage

A task the negative may attempt in both the first and second questioning periods is the establishment of certain disadvantages in the affirmative plan. For example, the negative may intend to assert that any method of representation chosen by the affirmative for a federal world union would prove unsatisfactory, questioning as follows:

Q. Is your union to be military in nature and ignore those economic matters that cause wars?

A. No, our union will consider economic matters too, and will take action where necessary.

Q. But the power of the union to enforce economic decisions will be rather weak, won't it?

A. Not at all. We intend to give our union full authority to go ahead on these matters.

[The witness at this point was laughing up his sleeve, thinking he had neatly stopped a possible negative attack on the grounds that the union would be powerless to deal with the economic causes of war. Actually, he had fallen into the trap set for him by the negative.]

Q. How do you intend to have the member nations of your union represented?

A. Well, by literate population probably. The number of representatives from each nation will be determined by the number of literate people in that country as determined by an international commission.

Q. You are definitely of the opinion that member nations will be represented in proportion to literate population of that country?

A. Yes, reasonably certain.

Q. What do you mean by "reasonably certain"? Is there any doubt about it?

A. No. We favor literate population.

Q. Definitely?

A. Yes, definitely.

Q. Do you know that half of the world's population is centered in China, Japan, and India?

A. There are a lot of people there, but they are mostly illiterate.

Q. Have you ever heard of the Soviet government's progress in overcoming illiteracy?

A. Yes, in general.

Q. Are you aware that in 1926, 50 per cent of the population of the Soviet Union was illiterate?

A. I knew the figure was high.

Q. And are you aware that in thirteen years prior to the war, the Soviet Union cut its illiteracy by two thirds?

A. I had heard something about it. Of course, we have only their word for it.

Q. Is it not true that China, Japan, and India, with half of the world's population, will dominate your union and thus rule the United States?

A. No, they have large populations, but as we said before, the people are mostly illiterate. That's why we chose the literate population method—it leaves the Western powers in control.

Q. But if China, India, and Japan become literate at the same rate as the Soviet Union, in thirteen years they will have overwhelming control of the union?

A. Yes, but only if they become literate at the same rate. We don't think they will.

Q. They would have every incentive for doing so, would they not?

A. Well, I don't know. I doubt if they would want more representation. They'll have too much reconstruction work at home.

Q. That is your basis for suggesting that they would not become literate as fast as Soviet Russia became literate?

A. Yes.

Q. By securing more representation these countries would control the union, would they not?

A. Yes, but we don't see why they would want to control the union. They'll have plenty of postwar reconstruction work to keep them busy at home without worrying about other countries.

Q. Since you mentioned earlier, in reply to a question, that one of the purposes of the union would be to direct economic matters, and since the giving of aid from the United States to China and India would certainly be an economic matter, China and India, by controlling the union, could direct that economic aid be sent to them regardless of the wishes of the United States, could they not?

A. That wasn't what we planned.

Q. But it could happen, couldn't it?

A. Yes, I suppose so.

Q. Then China and India would have a very strong incentive for becoming literate and thus controlling the union, wouldn't they?

A. Well . . . possibly.

Q. Why "possibly"?

A. Perhaps I shouldn't have said that. Yes, they would have a strong incentive.

Q. Then we can expect them to become literate at the earliest possible moment under this plan?

A. Yes.

Q. And the Soviet government, with no such incentive for outside aid, succeeded in its literacy program in only thirteen years?

A. Yes, if you can believe what they say.

Q. Then we can expect India and China to do it in even less time?

A. No, not less time. Maybe the same time.

Q. All right, then we can expect them to do it in the same time, thirteen years. So at the end of that time they will control the union?

A. Yes.

Q. And have the right to direct the amount of economic aid that the United States will send to them?

A. Perhaps.

Q. Thank you. No more questions.

Needless to say, questioning of this caliber requires much thought and practice. The order of questions is important, and the ability to think on one's feet is vital. Above all, however, is it necessary for the questions to be prepared in advance, with all contingencies anticipated and courses of action decided upon.

Unlike many debaters, the questioner in this case did not stop prematurely; he followed the line of questioning out to its logical conclusion, so that everyone could see what had been proved. Skipping from one topic to another in the questioning period is futile.

Sometimes one of the teams uncovers a unique advantage or disadvantage in one of the proposed plans. In the following example, the teams were debating, "Resolved, that the federal government should regulate by law all labor unions in the United States." The word "regulate" was officially defined to include, among other things, compulsory incorporation. The affirmative proposed as an advantage that incorporation would make union contracts binding. The affirmative team was prepared to show that this was desirable and that the affirmative plan would bring it about. The negative, taken by surprise, knew next to nothing about the legal aspects of the case. The affirmative capitalized on this surprise in its questioning periods. The following example, in which the affirmative forced the negative to concede the point, was accomplished by a skillful questioner against a witness who was caught off guard, but who was still hard to handle:

Q. Do you believe that it is desirable for labor unions to make binding contracts?

A. Well . . . I really don't have much of an opinion on that point. It doesn't seem relevant to the debate.

Q. You are opposing a program that requires the incorporation of labor unions?

A. Yes.

Q. And you are no doubt aware of the significance of incorporation on the legality of union contracts?

A. I don't think this debate topic is essentially a legal problem. You are trying to cloud the issues.

Q. To repeat the question in different words, are you aware that the incorporation of labor unions would make them legal entities capable of making contracts, which in turn would make their now-unenforcible contracts binding?

A. I don't think you care whether I am "aware" of your alleged fact or not.

Q. I'll phrase the question in another way. Do you agree or disagree that incorporation of labor unions would make their contracts legally binding?

A. Disagree.

Q. Have you any cases to support your position?

A. No.

Q. And you listened to my speech earlier in the debate when I cited several cases to support our claim that incorporation would make union contracts binding?

A. I heard it all right, but wasn't convinced.

Q. But you have no grounds on which to disagree?

A. No.

Q. Now that we finally seem to have agreed that the incorporation of labor unions would make their contracts binding, I'll repeat an earlier question: Do you believe it is desirable for labor unions to make binding contracts?

A. As I said before I don't think this should be a debate on the legal aspects of the problem.

Q. Yet you are opposing a program which requires the incorporation of labor unions?

A. Of course. If you heard the speech I just—

Q. And you are opposing that program even though you agreed a few moments ago that under this plan union contracts would be binding?

A. Yes. We certainly do oppose it.

Q. But you then about-face and say that the question of binding contracts is irrelevant?

A. No, I guess it's not irrelevant.

Q. Then what position does your team take?

A. We say it's not desirable for union contracts to be binding.

Q. Why?

A. Well, the unions would be oppressed.

Q. Would they be oppressed by being forced to live up to agreements into which they entered of their own free will?

A. Well, not exactly oppressed.

Q. The fact is, they would not be harmed at all, would they?

A. No, I suppose not.

Q. And the general public would gain?

A. You haven't proved that. You're assuming something.

Q. Is it true that most union contracts have no-strike clauses?

A. Yes.

Q. Does the public, in general, gain or lose by strikes?

A. It's hard to generalize.

Q. Is a strike of milk truck drivers, which prevents children from getting their milk, desirable from the standpoint of those who buy the milk?

A. No.

Q. Then the public loses by that strike?

A. Yes.

Q. And would similarly lose in other strikes which prevent the public from receiving the goods and services it desires?

A. Yes.

Q. Then to summarize, we agree that the affirmative plan, which provides for the incorporation of labor unions, would make union contracts binding?

A. Yes. I guess we have to agree to that.

Q. And we agree that unions would not be harmed by this provision?

A. Yes.

Q. And we agree that the general public would stand to gain by this provision?

A. Yes.

Q. Thank you. No more questions.

Building Up the Counterplan

In the usual form of Oregon style debate, each speaker, at the conclusion of his talk, is questioned by a member of the opposing team. Thus the first questioning period follows the first affirmative constructive speech. In this period, the negative may seek to build groundwork for its own case by securing admissions from the affirmative which support the as-yet-unknown negative counterplan.

An example of this type of questioning on the topic, "Resolved, that the United States should join in forming a permanent federal world union," follows. The negative intended to present as its strategic counterplan a program of out-and-out imperialism by the United States, in which the United States would control all of the important military bases of the world, including those now under the control of Great Britain, and in which the United States would allow Great Britain to function as a sub-empire.

This plan was chosen for its surprise value, but was extremely vulnerable on the ground that it would be unreasonable to expect Great Britain to submit to outside domination —she should not be required to permit anyone else to control British bases. The negative, however, reasoned that if it could trap the affirmative into admitting (1) that under the affirmative plan English policies would be under outside control, and (2) that under the affirmative plan the major British bases, such as Gibraltar, would be under outside control, the affirmative would not be in a position to object when the negative did the same thing in its counterplan. The technique by which the negative questioner accomplished this, in the face of stiff opposition from the witness, is shown below:

Q. You are recommending a federal world union?
A. Yes.
Q. Do you believe that your union will prevent future wars?
A. To a large extent, yes.
Q. Then you propose to put some teeth in the union, giving it the power to enforce its decisions?
A. Certainly, especially in regard to war and peace. Without that power the union would be helpless.

Q. Then you believe that the nations of the world should give up some of their national sovereignty?

A. I don't think I understand the question.

Q. Do you believe that the nations of the world should be subjected to some kind of control from outside their own country in order to prevent them from fighting each other?

A. Yes, that's exactly the point of the speech I just finished.

Q. And you include Germany and the Soviet Union, for instance, among those nations that will to a certain extent be controlled from outside?

A. Certainly.

Q. And England?

A. Yes, I suppose so. She'll be controlled enough to prevent her from waging war except in the interests of the union. But I don't think she'll want to wage war and so I don't think she'll need much control.

Q. But you propose to control all nations on the same basis, don't you?

A. All the countries who fought against the Axis will be on the same basis. Axis nations will be controlled more strictly. In Germany, for instance, we expect to—

Q. Thank you, that answers the question. Then Great Britain will be subjected to the same kind of control as the other Allies?

A. Yes.

Q. Why?

A. Well, we never can tell who might want to wage aggressive war in the future, so we have to play safe.

Q. I see. Then you'll want to control the use Great Britain makes of her important military bases, such as Gibraltar?

A. Yes, we will.

In this debate the questioner made no attempt, when he had secured the desired answers, to demonstrate the significance of these answers in the questioning period. Since he could accomplish that task properly only in a constructive speech after the negative counterplan had been presented, he wisely stopped questioning when he obtained the desired answers. This is one of the few instances in which it is desirable for the questioner to drop a line of questioning without showing its significance to the audience and judge.

It will be noted that one of the questions in the preceding series was, "Why?" Ordinarily, that is a bad question to ask; it opens the gates for a long-winded reply, and gives

the witness time to build up his own case at the expense
of the questioner. In this series an exception was made because everything the witness said supported the questioner's
position, and the questioner was prepared to interrupt if
necessary.

EXPOSING LACK OF RESEARCH

An effective line of questioning is to ask whether the witness is familar with a certain fact, or book, or law. If he
says that he is, the questioner can find out quickly whether
he is "fudging" or not. The witness can be made to look
rather bad if he is bluffing. On the other hand, if the witness
admits that he is not familiar with it, and he should be, he
can be made to look bad that way too.

Brooks Quimby [1] gives an excellent example:

Q. Are you familiar with the Pleven Plan?
A. No.
Q. You have never heard of the Pleven Plan to provide for a
unified defense of the free nations of Europe?
A. Yes, but—
Q. That is all I wanted to know. Thank you. If you wish to
explain, you will have opportunity in rebuttal. Are you
familiar with the Thomas Resolution?
A. No. I might recognize it if you explained it.
Q. Well, are you familiar with the Sparkman Resolution?
A. Not under that name.
Q. Let me put it this way: Are you familiar with the attempts
made in our Congress to revise the UN or to suggest such
revisions?
A. Oh, yes, I know about that.
Q. Then what specific objections do you have to the Thomas
Resolution?

If the opposition has been claiming that there are "lots of
examples" of a certain situation, and the questioner is reasonably sure that the witness is bluffing, he can ask:

Q. Would you please give three examples, and your sources?

This can be very powerful in the right spot. However,
like so many things, there is an element of risk. It is just

[1] Brooks Quimby, *So You Want to Discuss and Debate*, 2d ed. (Portland, Maine, J. Weston Walch, 1954), p. 139.

possible that the witness does have three examples! A safer, though less effective, method is to ask the same question in a constructive speech, so if the witness has a reply, he will have to give it on his own time.

When the Witness Doesn't Reply

If the witness says that he doesn't know the answer to the question, or if he just sits and doesn't say anything, the questioner has an opportunity to poke a little gentle fun. Here is one way:

Q. Mr. Frank, do you feel that the cost of this plan is important?

A. (Silence)

Q. Since Mr. Frank is unable to answer this question, we will go on to one much easier.

Another tack by which the same thing can be accomplished is this:

Q. Mr. Joessel, would you recommend that we continue to increase our storage facilities for farm surpluses?

A. (Silence)

Q. Has your team studied the question thoroughly enough to have an opinion, Mr. Joessel?

A. Well, yes, we have, but I think my partner should answer that question in his next speech.

Q. Are we to understand that your partner is informed on this phase of the problem but you are not?

Setting A Trap for the Questioner

The astute witness can set a trap for the questioner. One effective way is to hold back evidence until just the right moment. Brooks Quimby [2] gives this example:

Q. Do you claim that advertising reduces the unit cost of production?

A. Yes.

Q. Since this must be generally true to be significant, can you give proof of your statement?

A. Arrow collars are an example.

[2] *Ibid.*, p. 140.

Q. But you gave that one example already; have you any additional evidence to show that such an effect is general?
A. Certainly. Here is a book by Professor Starch of Harvard University, a well-known authority on advertising. On page 392 he has a long list of such cases. I shall be glad to read them to you. (Reads)
Q. All right, that is enough. Now—
A. I have a lot more if you want them.

TURNING THE TABLES

Sometimes the questioner can turn the tables, showing that the proposed solution aggravates the very problem it is supposed to solve. Needless to say, thorough analysis of the topic is needed before this can be done successfully. The following illustration [3] is from a debate on the topic, "Resolved, that the federal government should adopt a permanent program of wage and price control."

Q. Miss Smith, what is the purpose of price controls?
A. To keep prices down, of course.
Q. What made them high?
A. Lots of money in people's hands, a great demand, and a limited supply of goods.
Q. All right, let's consider those points. Are controls intended to decrease the amount of money in people's hands?
A. No.
Q. Or to reduce the demand?
A. No.
Q. Or are they intended to increase the supply of goods?
A. No. Controls control.
Q. That is, they don't deal with the causes of the situation at all, do they? They simply force buyers and sellers to accept prices lower than those prevailing on the free market?
A. Yes.
Q. All right, now let's take an example to see what happens. If you were thinking about buying a car, but weren't sure whether you wanted to or not, would the price help you make your decision?
A. Of course.
Q. That is, if you found a second-hand Plymouth you liked for $500, you might decide to buy it; but if the same car were $1000, you might decide to walk or ride the bus?

[3] The questions were suggested by Frank Chodorov's *One Is a Crowd* (New York, Devin-Adair, 1952), p. 83-8.

A. Yes, that's quite true.

Q. So the demand for goods is greater when they are low priced?

A. Certainly.

Q. Then price controls, by keeping prices fictitiously low and thus increasing demand, aggravate the very problem they are supposed to solve?

A. Well, I don't know that that would be true in every situation.

Q. But it would be true in the automobile situation?

A. Yes.

Q. And in other situations where the facts are essentially the same?

A. Yes.

Q. Very good. Now let's consider a little different aspect of the problem. Miss Smith, why do people work?

A. There are lots of reasons, but one of the most important is to make money.

Q. Most people do not work just for their health?

A. They certainly do not.

Q. They work to make money?

A. Yes.

Q. And if they find they aren't making much money, they sometimes look for something else to do?

A. Yes.

Q. Do you feel that way too?

A. Surely. Money isn't everything, but it's certainly important.

Q. If you were a dressmaker, and the government set a price for your dresses that was below your cost, what would you do?

A. I'd quit making dresses.

Q. Unless you reluctantly accepted illegal prices for those dresses, forced upon you by women who disregarded the law?

A. Yes.

Q. Suppose the government let you make a little profit, but not as much as you could make as a secretary?

A. I'd be tempted to be a secretary.

Q. If you stopped making dresses, would there be more or fewer dresses on the market?

A. Fewer, of course.

Q. Can we agree, then, that price controls tend to reduce the supply of goods and therefore aggravate the very problem they are supposed to solve?

A. (Silence)

Q. All right, Miss Smith, I won't press for an answer. I realize it could be embarrassing. Miss Smith, are you familiar with the meat-packing industry?

A. In a general way.

Q. Is it true that just about every part of the animal is put to some use, even the hair and the blood?

A. Yes, so I've heard.

Q. Is it true that when a pig is slaughtered, there are literally hundreds of commercial transactions before the pork chop reaches your grocery store and the hide reaches your glove shop?

A. I wouldn't be surprised.

Q. Would you agree then, Miss Smith, that there would be quite a number of points at which prices would need to be fixed and surveillance maintained?

A. Oh, yes.

Q. When we were discussing the dressmaking situation a few moments ago, I think we agreed that both buyer and seller might be tempted to disregard the law?

A. Yes.

Q. So enforcement agents will be necessary?

A. Yes.

Q. Would it be wrong to estimate that the number of government agents needed for *rigid* enforcement would come to at least a tenth of our population?

A. Well, that estimate sounds high.

Q. And, judging from some of the things that have come to light in FHA, the Internal Revenue Service, and other places, would you agree that someone is needed to watch the enforcement agents?

A. Yes, to some extent.

Q. Would the withdrawal of all these men from productive work increase or decrease the supply of goods?

A. Well, it would tend to decrease production somewhat.

Q. So here again, price controls aggravate the very problem they are supposed to solve? This time by diverting men from productive work to non-productive government employment?

A. Perhaps to a limited extent.

Q. Can we agree, then, that price controls make the problem worse in three ways? First, they increase demand by keeping prices fictitiously low. Second, they decrease supply by reducing the profit incentive and encouraging people to go into other more profitable activities. Third, they further reduce supplies of goods by diverting people from productive work to non-productive police work. Can we agree on those conclusions?

A. (Silence)

Q. Thanks. That's all. No more questions.

5

STRATEGY

Why do first-rate debating teams often use strategy? And why do the educators and speech teachers who, a few years ago, condemned strategy as unethical now accept and in some cases enthusiastically recommend its use?

The answers to these questions are not hard to find. The better debating teams use strategy because it gives them a distinct edge over their opponents. Educators and speech teachers like its emphasis on original thought and its tendency to develop the ability to adapt one's thinking processes to the exigencies of the moment.

Of course, it must not be assumed that such sentiments are unanimous. There are intelligent debaters who do not like strategy. There are educators who believe it out of place. But whether one chooses to use strategy or not, he needs to understand it, for without such knowledge he would find himself helpless at the hands of a team employing it.

What is strategy? The definitions of the past twenty years agree on one point—surprise and strategy somehow go together. An unexpected affirmative plan is certainly strategic. An unexpected negative counterplan is strategic. Unexpected advantages or disadvantages in the proposed plans are strategic. A trap is strategic. Does strategy include anything else? One of the country's top teachers of speech and debating [1] has this to say:

> To me, the essential elements in strategy are the finesse and ingenuity in which we package our logic and evidence like cellophane and pretty ribbons. Maybe my definition should be simply good and rather smart audience and opposition psychology.

In this book we shall employ this broad definition.

[1] Dr. Hugo Hellman, Director of the School of Speech, Marquette University.

Types of Debating

The alternative to strategic debating is conventional debating. Conventional debating consists of presenting the plan generally discussed in the handbooks and newspapers, or something close to it. The plan is supported by the usual evidence, plus any additional evidence that the debater is able to dig up. The team hopes, by putting the known facts together in a more convincing manner, to overpower the opposition.

Strategic debating generally consists of presenting some new approach to the topic not found in the handbooks, supported by new or old evidence. The debaters attempt to choose a plan or a set of advantages that are inherently just as sound as the usual ones, but which have the added advantage of being completely unexpected by the other team.

In both conventional and strategic debating the teams attempt to support their cases with so much evidence, such logical reasoning, and with such clear organization of thought that the opposing team is unable to tear down the line of argument. Both types of debating require considerable library research. Strategic debating, however, places more emphasis on constructive, original thought by the debater since he is required to discover a new approach to the problem. Intelligent debaters like strategy better and use it more than their less brilliant colleagues, probably for this reason.

The use of strategy is not new. As long ago as 1914, E. R. Nichols [2] pointed out many of the possibilities.

> Among the special styles or systems the surprise debate is most noteworthy. A surprise debate is, naturally, one which catches opponents off-guard, or napping, which presents them with a course of reasoning or with some striking or effective argument which in preparing for the debate they have entirely overlooked. A surprise, then, is any departure from the conventional or accepted argument which is of importance. The side springing the surprise hopes to gain the jump on opponents during the first few moments of bewilderment while they are floundering around and casting about for an answer. Inability to summon some answer

---

[2] E. R. Nichols, Introduction to his *Intercollegiate Debates* (New York, Hinds, Noble, and Eldredge, 1914), v. 4, p. xiv-xx.

to a surprise argument is usually fatal, that is, if the surprise
argument is in the least vital or important in settling the issues
of the debate. This last qualifying clause, as all will recognize,
makes genuine surprise difficult to find.

The principle strategic approaches are (1) the presentation of an unexpected plan or counterplan, (2) the presentation of an unexpected advantage or disadvantage in the
conventional proposal, (3) the acceptance of the negative
counterplan by the affirmative in the middle of the debate,
(4) the use of traps of various kinds, and (5) the use of
those forms of judge, audience, and opposition psychology
that are not based on surprise. These will be discussed in
turn.

Unexpected Proposals

Professor William H. Davis [3] pointed out in 1915 an example of the use of an unexpected plan by the negative:

> A certain debate was held on the subject, "Resolved, that county
> elections in the various states should conform to the principles of
> the short ballot." It was assumed by all that the negative would
> support the *status quo* in county political organization. They did
> not. Instead, they favored the complete abolition of county gov-
> ernment as we understand it. . . . I submit that the contention
> of the negative, justifying as it does a vote of *no* on the resolu-
> tion, was in order.

Today the use of an unexpected case has become so
widely understood that almost no one denies its propriety,
so long as the teams stick to the proposition—that is, so
long as the proposal is not one that would be ruled out of
order in a legislative assembly.

Of course, just as a football team must mix its plays,
the debating team must use both conventional and unusual
cases so that the opposition is kept guessing; otherwise the
"unusual" case is expected, and there is no surprise. The
fundamental principle behind strategic debating is that the
opposing team must be caught off guard, thus being forced

to meet the most difficult case possible. Of course, the most difficult case to meet in a debate is one for which the team is not prepared.

Both affirmative and negative teams can find unique plans in a properly worded resolution; a few examples illustrate the point.

In a debate on the topic, "Resolved, that the federal government should provide a system of complete medical care available to all citizens at public expense," most affirmative teams would recommend the usual mild plan for a government program which would exist along side the present system of private medicine, supported by the federal treasury. If, however, the affirmative wants to catch its opposition off guard, it can recommend that private medicine be abolished completely to avoid unnecessary duplication, and that the program be supported by a national lottery or a special federal sales tax, whichever happens to appeal to the affirmative team. And since the negative will probably point out the opposition of the American Medical Association, the affirmative might steal a little of the negative's thunder by having the AMA administer the new federal program. Doubtless other ideas along this line will occur to the debater.

In a debate on the topic, "Resolved, that labor should be given a direct share in the management of industry," most affirmative teams would probably recommend that labor, especially labor unions, be given a greater voice in establishing company policies. If the affirmative would like to see a surprised look on the faces of the opposing debaters, it might recommend that the "share" be 100 per cent, that present owners be ousted entirely, and that industry be run solely for the financial benefit of the workers, thus encouraging more efficient work, which in turn could result in lower prices.

The case which the general public considers unusual may, however, be anticipated by the team's opponents if they happen to hear about it. When a "surprise" case becomes known before the debate, it may be more of a liability than an asset, and under such circumstances another case can be substituted with remarkable effectiveness. Professor E. R. Nichols [4] gave the following example in 1914:

> A few years ago Baker University lost a debate to Ottawa University on the federal income tax because the plan of assessment and collection was not the one they expected the Ottawa affirmative to propose. Instead of putting up a novel and unique plan which had been devised at one of the universities for debating purposes, but which, since it was getting to be well known, the Ottawa men had reason to expect the Baker men would be prepared to meet, they proposed the English plan of stoppage at the source. As was expected the Baker team had a carefully prepared speech all ready for the university's novel plan of assessment and collection. The Ottawa debaters had the pleasure of pointing out, as they had planned to do, that the Baker team was hammering a straw man and had not touched their plan. The debate was lost before the Baker men could readjust themselves.

Harlan [5] points out this example from his own experience:

> It is oftentimes highly desirable to change horses in the middle of a season. The most sensational and advantageous use of this strategy is in the middle of a tournament. Most tournaments allow scouting and use coaches for judges. By the second day of such a tournament every team there knows what every other team has. And if there is anything new, everyone is working on a refutation to meet it. . . .

> [One year we were] debating the Supreme Court question. We went through the first day with a plan on both sides of the question to use a referendum direct to the people. We did not lose a debate the first day. That night every alert team with its coach sat up late working on arguments against the referendum, for they had not heard of it being used until they came to the tournament. Early the next morning we met a crack team from Louisiana. They were ready for the referendum. They anticipated it in their speeches from the start, and battled away against it. We came calmly forth in the last part of our second speech with an entirely new plan; that of using the state legislature as a final check. We then proceeded to laugh at our opponents for guessing wrong, related to the judges just how and why we had shifted positions, and won debates all day.

[4] E. R. Nichols, Introduction to his *Intercollegiate Debates* (New York, Hinds, Noble, and Eldridge, 1914), v. 4, p. xiv-xxv.

[5] R. E. Harlan, *Strategic Debating* (Boston, Chapman & Grimes, 1940), p. 42, 43.

Unexpected Advantages and Disadvantages

Presentation of an unexpected plan of action is not the only way that surprise, and thus strategy, can be achieved. A team may present an expected, commonplace plan, but may present an advantage or disadvantage that was not anticipated. For example, many debates were held on the regulation of labor unions, including compulsory incorporation, before a student who happened to be taking a course in the law of contracts decided that incorporation would be an advantage because under it union contracts would be made legally binding. This is strictly a legal question, with cases to be cited on both sides. Investigation revealed cases where union contracts were held to be binding even though the union was unincorporated, and other cases were found where union contracts were held to be unenforcible because the unincorporated union was not a legal entity and was not capable of making contracts. Since the point was new, the team introducing it had a tremendous advantage; it could prove the point either way, while the opposition was forced to accept whatever conclusions the strategic team drew. This is an example of surprise secured by means of a new advantage for an old plan, rather than through a new and unexpected plan.

Acceptance of Counterplan

The use of a counterplan by the negative has already been considered in other chapters, and will not be discussed again here. The counterplan is simply a substitute proposal offered by the negative in place of the affirmative proposal. The negative, in effect, takes the position that the affirmative plan should not be adopted because it would interfere with the adoption of another, superior plan — namely, the one offered by the negative.

Now obviously if the negative's case is to hold water, the counterplan must be entirely different from, and inconsistent with, the affirmative plan. Otherwise the affirmative's plan can (and possibly should) still be adopted even if the negative's plan is admittedly good. This is the basis for an effective bit of strategy by the affirmative.[6]

Suppose that the affirmative is recommending that the federal government adopt Plan A. The negative disputes this, claiming that a more satisfactory solution would be the adoption of Plan C. The negative, being an inexperienced team, neglects to make Plan C inconsistent with Plan A.

The affirmative then can make the negative team fully aware of its deficiencies by agreeing that Plan C should be adopted, that is, by accepting the negative proposal as part of its own plan.

This takes all the wind from the sails of the negative. It has devoted a great deal of time to Plan C, and since that plan no longer has anything to do with the main question (whether Plan A should be adopted or not), the time has been entirely wasted. The debate then boils down to a discussion of the merits of Plan A, and in a contest of this kind the affirmative, having had considerably more speaking time to devote to the subject, will almost certainly win.

It will be remembered that there is a well-established debating rule which prohibits any revision of position of either team during the progress of the debate. In applying the strategy outlined here, the affirmative must be careful not to violate this rule. The affirmative should take the attitude that it liked Plan C all along, but didn't consider it worth mentioning earlier, since it was irrelevant to the debate until the negative brought it up. In this way the affirmative can protect itself against a possible negative charge that the various affirmative speakers were not consistent, that they shifted ground in the middle of the debate.

TRAPS

There are several varieties of traps in debating. Ordinarily the intention is to lead the opposing team into a dilemma or an inconsistency, and then to expose it for public

[6] This and the corresponding strategy used by the negative team are described in my article, "Some Unfamiliar Strategy," *Debater's Magazine*, 2:14-48, March 1946. The article gives a more detailed account than is possible here.

scrutiny. This is supposed to impress the judge with the illogical thinking of the other team, and if the inconsistency is of sufficient importance, it may do just that.

Traps may be developed in questioning, either in Oregon style debate or by asking direct questions in the constructive speeches.

Almost every debate topic offers possibilities if the debater cares to exercise his ingenuity.

An effective trap was used by the team which won the Ohio high school championship a few years ago. They were debating the affirmative of the federal world union question. They anticipated, naturally enough, that the negative would contend that Russia would not join a world government, and that any attempt to set one up would only widen the split between the East and the West.

Before the negative had a chance to bring up this argument, the affirmative asked a direct question, "Do you believe that Russia's intentions are peaceful?" The negative, not knowing what the affirmative intended to do with this information, hedged; it pointed out many warlike acts by Russia and some peaceful acts, concluding that no one knows what Russia's intentions are.

Later in the debate, when the negative claimed that Russia would not join the union (and therefore the split between East and West would be widened), the affirmative calmly pointed out that since by the negative's own admission no one knows what Russia's intentions are, the negative is hardly justified in asserting that Russia would not join the union. The affirmative's conclusion was that the negative argument simply couldn't be considered established.

PSYCHOLOGICAL DEVICES

Some psychological devices, appropriately classified as strategy, do not contain the element of surprise. Such techniques are intended, as pointed out by Hellman, to package our logic and evidence with cellophane and pretty ribbons.

The most obvious technique, of course, is to appeal to any known prejudices of the audience and judge. Is this ethical? Whether the reader's answer be *yes* or *no,* it is certainly used in nearly every speech one hears, on or off the debate platform. We must not suppose the debater so naïve as to be unaware of the possibility. Generally it is called "adapting the speech to the audience" or "persuasion." If the judge is a minister from some church which frowns upon liquor, and if the debater is opposing unicameral legislatures, he can find and use some instance when the presence of a second house prevented some objectionable liquor bill from going through. His logic would be just as convincing if he used some other illustration, but the impact on the judge might not be as great.

Another technique is the use of visual aids—maps, charts, graphs, even big cardboard signs with an outline of the team's case. Again, the logic is the same whether such aids are used or not, but the chance of the arguments sinking in is greater when they are used.

A third technique is the intimidation of the opposing team. Not physical intimidation, of course, but mental intimidation. One can see that the opposing team finds out how many opponents have been defeated in the past few months, how many tournaments have been won, and favorable comments of past judges. The idea is, as Harlan expresses it, to give the opposition the impression that if the team is half as good as it appears to be the debate is already over. And with that start, it *is* over.

Still another device is the dramatized "air of disappointment." When the opposition is a team whose arguments can be anticipated with fair degree of accuracy, and when the debater has a sense of humor that can sting without leaving a welt, he can poke a little gentle fun at the use of minor stock arguments in a rebuttal speech something like this:

> As my colleague mentioned in his first speech, ladies and gentlemen, we had hopes that this debate would not descend to name-calling and reactionary platitudinizing, which are the property of the unthinking man on the street and housewives gossiping over the back fence. We had hopes that we could discuss this question on important social and political issues, that we could justify

the money spent on our college education by discussing this matter logically and intelligently. But what has happened? Our fond hopes have been dashed to pieces. The gentlemen from Siwash, an institution noted for its intellectual endeavors, have come here to debate and instead have resurrected the old hash and ancient drivel about. . . . I am sure that you are as disappointed as I am, ladies and gentlemen, and I am quite hopeful that the gentlemen of the negative, who I know are honest and capable debaters, will bury what they have so unfortunately resurrected and come forward to meet us squarely for the rest of the debate on the important issues.[7]

The debater will find it both enjoyable and instructive to practice reading the preceding paragraph aloud until he has just the right touch. Then he will know how it feels to have the debate in the palm of his hand—the goal of all real debate strategy.

LIMITS OF STRATEGY

It is probably safe to say that nearly everyone concerned with debating agrees that some strategy is permissible; this position has been reflected in the various writings since 1914. However, it is also true that somewhere there must be limits; where are they?

Of the various types of strategy possible, the surprise case has caused the most controversy and is in greatest need of careful delimitation. Probably the most universally acceptable position would be this:

The teams are permitted to recommend any plan permitted by the proposition, whether it be a surprise or not. The teams, however, are not permitted to recommend a plan that would be considered out of order in a legislative assembly discussing that proposition.

It must be recognized that such a dividing line is hazy at best. Earlier in this chapter, Davis justified a certain surprise counterplan on the grounds that it justified a vote of *no* on the resolution, and therefore would be in order in a legislative assembly or in a debate. Yet at least one highly

[7] I am indebted to Glenn H. Leggett, formerly coach of debate at the Massachusetts Institute of Technology, for this material.

respected debate coach has taken the position that this particular counterplan would not be permissible, because it would be ruled out of order in a legislative assembly. When two competent persons, using the same criterion, arrive at opposite conclusions from a given illustration, it is easy to see why there is controversy about the extent to which strategy may go.

EDUCATIONAL ASPECTS

Since debate is primarily an educational activity, the educational values of strategy may be examined.

One point of view is that the use of surprise cases may avoid a discussion of the real issues which must be decided in determining a solution to the problem inherent in the proposition, and if so, the debate ceases to be an educational experience. The conclusion is that it is preferable for the teams to support the conventional cases.

The objection to this point of view is that any artificial limitation in the scope of the debate (by "artificial" is meant any limitation not imposed by the proposition itself) is likely to exclude cases which sound ridiculous on the surface but which are fundamentally sound.

An example of this may be found in the first published discussion of strategy (1914), in which E. R. Nichols pointed out one team's use of a "trick case" on the income tax question. That team recommended, as a surprise, that the amount of the income tax be withheld from the employee's wages. Today the United States Government is doing just exactly that. The plan that was a "trick case" in 1914 is in operation today.

Here is the point: Plans that seem radical and tricky may be closer to the true solution (if such a thing exists) than the commonly known proposals. Who is to decide which plans the teams must avoid discussing? Surely no one except the teams themselves, for otherwise they might not be permitted to use perfectly sound plans within the scope of the proposition. A fundamentally unsound plan takes a beating when pitted against capable opposition, and any thinking team avoids it like toothache.

The point of view to which the present work subscribes is that the educational values of debate are at least as great, perhaps greater, when surprise cases are judiciously used, on the following grounds:

First: The educational benefits of debate are greater when the participants work harder, and they work harder in a competitive atmosphere. This atmosphere is encouraged by the occasional use of surprise cases. When a team gets thrashed because it failed to prepare to refute some little-known plan, is it more likely to keep on making the same mistake or to prepare more thoroughly in the future?

Second: Written or memorized speeches are not possible when meeting a surprise case, and thus the ability to speak extemporaneously, yet to the point and with logic, is developed.

Third: More extensive research is encouraged. The team preparing the surprise must go beyond the handbook stage, while the team using the conventional case may or may not. Opponents must work harder, too, even if they are not preparing a surprise of their own. More research is required to prepare to refute several possible cases (including the conventional one) than only one possibility.

Fourth: Considerable thought must be given by the debater to the basic issues and to the various possible solutions when he develops his own surprise case. This is not always true when the debater recites a widely-publicized plan, with merits and demerits which have already been discovered and analyzed by others.

It is not necessary to assert that debating teams *must* or even *should* use surprise cases the majority of the time. That is a matter of individual team preference. But the teams do have the *right* to use surprise cases, and the right to instruction in the use of such cases.

6

JUDGING

The basic concepts employed by the debate judge were outlined in Chapter 1. It will be recalled that

The team doing the better debating is the winner (**9 a**)

The judge's job is to decide which team did the "better debating" in that particular contest.

PRELIMINARIES

The necessary materials—pencils and lined paper—are usually provided by the host, but some judges prefer to provide their own in case the host's materials are forgotten or unsuitable. A pocket notebook is seldom sufficient for this purpose.

Before the speeches start, the judge may find it advisable to write down the exact wording of the topic, to serve as a reference in case the teams conflict in their interpretation of the proposition. The names of the speakers may also be recorded, so the judge can refer to them by name in his critique, and so he can identify them if they refer to each other by name.

As a gesture of courtesy, some judges make it a point to meet the two coaches before the debate. Any such contacts must be strictly impartial, of course; before the debate begins, the judge finds a seat apart from the coaches.

These preliminaries over, he can sit back, relax, and enjoy the contest.

Two techniques are currently used to determine which team did the "better debating," either of which may be employed successfully by the judge.

Method 1: The Score Sheet

The score sheet method of judging consists of

(1) preparing a list of the elements of effective debating,
(2) assigning an arbitrary weight or value to each,
(3) rating each team (or each speaker) on each element, and
(4) totaling the points and awarding the decision to the team with the highest total.

The procedure is similar to that used in judging boxing matches, except that the debate judge scores by elements instead of by rounds.

As might be expected, considerable differences are found between forms prepared for this purpose. Quite naturally, each author prefers his own list and his own point system. It would be very difficult to say that one score sheet is better than another, since it is simply a matter of opinion.

Here are some score sheets in current use:

Example 1

Speech Activities, inside back cover, Spring 1953.

Skill in analysis ....10 to 20 points per speaker
Adequacy of organization ....Same
Knowledge of subject ....Same
Presentation of evidence .....Same
Use of reasoning ....Same
Refutation and rebuttal ......Same
Style of presentation ....Same
Ethical considerations ....Same
                              ——
                              Total

Example 2

James H. McBurney, James M. O'Neill, and Glen E. Mills, in *Argumentation and Debate* (New York, Macmillan Company, 1951) page 282.

Analysis and case ....1 to 5 points per speaker
Attack and defense ....Same
Evidence ....Same
Delivery ....Same
                            ——
                            Total

Example 3

Waldo W. Braden and Earnest Brandenburg, *Oral Decision-Making* (New York, Harper, 1955) page 522.

Analysis ....1 to 5 points per team
Organization ....Same
Argument and facts ....Same
Refutation ....Same
Language ....Same
Delivery ....Same
Attitudes ....Same
Over-all effectiveness ....Same
                                    ——
                                    Total

Example 4

Eugene C. Chenoweth, *Discussion and Debate* (Dubuque, Iowa, W. C. Brown Company, 1951) page 328.

Analysis ....1 to 5 points per speaker
Evidence ....Same
Argument ....Same
Organization ....Same
Adaptation ....Same
Refutation-rebuttal ....Same
Use of language ....Same
Delivery ....Same
Persuasion ....Same
                                    ——
                                    Total

Example 5

Eugene C. Chenoweth, *Discussion and Debate* (Dubuque, Iowa, W. C. Brown Company, 1951) page 328.

Evidence ....1 to 3 points per speaker
Argument ....Same
Organization ....Same
Refutation ....Same
Rebuttal ....Same
Delivery ....Same
                                    ——
                                    Total

Sometimes the host gives the judge a prepared score sheet, so the judge does not have to bear the entire responsibility for some rather arbitrary decisions.

The score sheet technique has been in use for many years and, despite its reliance on personal opinion, it can be of help, particularly in the case of judges who are not prepared to keep track of the arguments and their refutation through to the conclusion of the debate.

Method 2: The Double Summary

Double summary judging consists of following the arguments and awarding the decision to the team which succeeds in doing what the proposition requires.

The judging procedure consists of

(1) recording the advantages brought out by the affirmative,

(2) recording the disadvantages brought out by the negative,

(3) recording the refutation and counter-refutation,

(4) determining which advantages and disadvantages remain standing at the end of the debate, and

(5) awarding the decision to the team which succeeds in doing what the proposition requires.

It will be recognized at once that this technique requires an alert judge, but if he does his job, the decision is sound and objective, with a minimum of reliance on personal opinion.

Recording the Arguments In a Status Quo Debate

It might be helpful to review, in a little more detail, the judge's procedure in a typical debate, when using the double-summary technique.

First, he prepares two sheets of paper, one for the affirmative case and one for the negative case. Blank paper with a few ruled lines will do very nicely.

On the affirmative sheet, the judge records the plan's advantages, as brought out by the affirmative. On the negative sheet, he records the plan's disadvantages, as brought out by the negative.

Advantages

Resolved, that the federal government should initiate a policy of free trade among nations friendly to the United States.

	Affirmative	Negative	Affirmative	Negative
1	Would improve our standard of living—more goods at lower prices			
2	Would improve our foreign relations—our tariffs are forcing friends to trade with USSR	Friends must not be very much interested in trading with us—their controls are tighter than ours		
3				
4				

Disadvantages

	Negative	Affirmative	Negative	Affirmative
1	Would produce unemployment, due to lower wage scales and that would mean higher taxes for those still employed	Each country would mfg the goods it is best qualified to produce. Furthermore, tariffs can also displace workers.		
2	Would lower farm incomes—meat and grain would be dumped here	On contrary, exports are vital to farmers, and we can't expect to export without providing means of payment.		
3	Would weaken US militarily—forced to shut down essential war industries: tungsten, mining. And lose essential skills	We would protect essential war industries. Not true—expert testimony.	Where would this stop? Everything is essential	Policy and mechanica explained satisfactorily.
4	Would prevent development of new industries if someone else happened to have the lead	Would have 20-year protection for infant industries		

Since many methods of case organization are possible in debate, the judge finds its necessary to convert the arguments, using some kind of common denominator for purposes of comparison. Thus, instead of recording whatever one team happens to consider a "point":

The judge records only advantages and disadvantages in the proposed plan, and the refutation of such arguments.

It makes no difference how the teams organize their cases; sooner or later the advantages and disadvantages are bound to come out. The judge must be alert, for they may appear under different labels.

As each argument is refuted, successfully, the judge records the refutation opposite the original argument.

Then, if the original argument is rebuilt, the judge records that, too, opposite the refutation. One argument may be tossed back and forth several times before it comes to rest.

Status quo debate. Example 1

Let's see how this works in a very simple debate:

> *He*: Let's go to the Bijou. That comedy ought to be good.
>   (Advantage: Enjoyment of comedy.)
>
> *She*: Oh, let's not. Ruth says it isn't so good, and you know how that popcorn smells.
>   (Advantage refuted. Disadvantage: Smell of popcorn.)

The decision would go to the negative. No advantages were established, and one disadvantage remained standing. The affirmative failed to show that its plan would be better than the *status quo,* and therefore failed in its burden of proof.

Status quo debate. Example 2

Now, let's look at another example:

> *Husband*: Sweetheart, what do you say we trade the old car in on a new one? Our repair bills are terrific.
>   (Advantage: Reduction in repair bills.)

Wife: But dear, how can we afford it? You know the house needs painting and the children need new clothes and besides, you promised me a new coat.
(Disadvantage: Lack of capital; available capital required for other purposes.)

Husband: Well, I was talking to Joe Barnes down at the garage and he says we could swing it for $65 a month.
(Refutation of the "lack of capital" argument.)

Wife: Now, Jim, you know after that last time, you promised we wouldn't buy anything else on credit, and as for repairs, Sarah says new cars need lots of repairs too.
(Rebuilding of "lack of capital" disadvantage. Refutation of "reduction in repair bills" advantage.)

Here again the decision would go to the negative. At the end of the debate, the judge could readily note, from his double-summary sheets, that no advantages remained standing and one disadvantage was established. The affirmative failed to show that its plan would offer an improvement over the *status quo,* and therefore the negative won.

RECORDING THE ARGUMENTS
IN A COUNTERPLAN DEBATE

The negative team, of course, does not need to support the *status quo* unless it chooses to do so; it may prefer to offer a counterplan instead.

We have already reviewed what the judge does in a *status quo* debate. Now let's see what happens in a counter-plan debate.

When the debate starts, the judge, of course, has no idea which position the negative will take. He prepares his double summary sheets on the assumption that this will be a *status quo* debate. During the first affirmative speech he records the plan's advantages as brought out in that speech.

Later, probably during the first negative speech, the judge may discover that the negative intends to support a counterplan.

The sheets he started (affirmative plan *versus status quo*) are now irrelevant, so he discards them and starts a new set.[1]

The new sheets show the counterplan *versus* the affirmative plan. He records the counterplan's advantages on one sheet and the affirmative plan's disadvantages on the other sheet.

Once these sheets have been prepared, the judge follows the debate exactly as he would a *status quo* debate, the only difference being that the negative now has the burden of proof.

Counterplan debate. Example

Let's see how this works out in a simple counterplan debate:

He: Say, why don't we go to the Bijou tonight? That comedy ought to be good.
  (Advantage: Enjoyment of comedy.)
She: Oh, wouldn't you rather go swimming? It's so hot tonight and it would be cooler at the pool.
  (Recommendation of counterplan. The judge discards his first set of sheets and starts a new set. Advantage of counterplan: Cooler at the pool.)
He: Jim said the chlorine system isn't working and it's pretty bad at the pool this week. And the Bijou is air conditioned.
  (Disadvantage of counterplan: Chlorine system defective. Refutation of the "cooler" advantage.)
She: Well, I thought it would be nice to go swimming.

Regardless of where they went that night ("Never underestimate the power of a woman"), the debate itself was won by the affirmative.

If the above arguments are charted, it will quickly be seen that the negative failed to establish any advantages for its counterplan.

[1] Theoretically, there might be a fly in the judge's ointment. Conceivably, the negative could offer a counterplan without admitting that the affirmative's proposal is better than the *status quo*. This would require the judge to maintain both sets of sheets at the same time.

In practice, this stand is exceedingly rare. When the negative offers a counterplan, it admits that the *status quo* is bad, either expressly or by implication. It is too confusing for the negative to take any other stand. This is fortunate, for it keeps things simple for the judge.

The affirmative did establish one defect in the counter-plan (a bad chlorine situation at the pool).

The affirmative successfully demonstrated that its plan would be better than the counterplan, so the affirmative gets the decision.

The reader can readily appreciate how confusing this cross-fire of arguments might be in a full hour's debate if not written down in organized form. In self-protection, the judge needs to chart the arguments. It's not hard if he keeps track as he goes, and at the end of the debate a quick review will show him how matters stand, if he simply notes which blocks are filled in and which are vacant.

DECIDING WHAT ARGUMENTS TO ACCEPT

The task of the judge during the debate is more than one of simple record keeping. Before he knows whether to accept and record an argument or not, he must consider the supporting evidence and logic presented by the debater.

An argument is considered established if supported by enough evidence and logic to convince an intelligent but previously uninformed person that it is more reasonable to believe the assertion than to disbelieve it (5 b).

Considerable significance should be attached to the phrase "previously uninformed." It means:

The judge must base his decision entirely on the material presented, without regard for other material which he may happen to possess (9 d).

Since the judge is deciding which of the two teams did the better job of debating, and not the "truth" inherent in the topic:

The judge is required to accept as true all arguments backed by reasonable proof (as defined above) until such arguments are overthrown by the opposing team (9 e).

The judge must not accept ideas which are not backed by reasonable proof (9 f).

As each constructive argument is attacked by the opposition, the judge asks himself whether the attempt at refutation was successful. If so, the judge records the refutation. If not, the original argument stands until overthrown.

Some criticisms of debate judging have arisen from well-meaning attempts on the part of judges to evaluate the evidence presented; such an evaluation may easily alienate those whose personal convictions are overruled. Furthermore, such an "evaluation" is too often nothing more than a simple expression of the judge's own personal beliefs on the subject. Evaluation of evidence is the job of the debaters; the judge had best stay out of it.

REACHING THE DECISION

At the conclusion of the debate, the judge analyzes his notes. He considers only the arguments which remain standing at the end of the debate, *i.e.,* those for which satisfactory refutation has not been offered, or which were rebuilt satisfactorily after refutation.

He then arrives at the decision on the following basis:

A. In *status quo* debates:

1. The plan is shown by the teams to have some advantages and no disadvantages at all:
   Decision: Affirmative

2. The plan is shown to have no advantages of any kind:
   Decision: Negative

3. The plan is shown to have both advantages and disadvantages:
   Decision: Either team, depending on (1) the demonstrated importance of the advantages and disadvantages, and (2) the quantity.

B. In counterplan debates:

1. The counterplan is shown to have advantages and no disadvantages with respect to the affirmative proposal:
   Decision: Negative

2. The counterplan is shown to have no advantages with respect to the affirmative proposal:
   Decision: Affirmative

3. The counterplan is shown to have both advantages and disadvantages with respect to the affirmative proposal: *Decision:* Either team, depending on (1) the demonstrated importance of the established advantages and disadvantages, and (2) the quantity.

Until the judge is thoroughly familiar with judging technique, he may find it helpful to take a copy of the above chart with him to the debate, for quick reference.

TIES

It should be evident, after a few moments' consideration, that a tie in debating is impossible. Sometimes such a decision is announced, but it can only reflect on the ability of the judge. Under every conceivable circumstance, there is some good reason for awarding the decision to one team.

As an example, assume that both teams have established part of their cases. The affirmative has succeeded in showing that its plan will bring about certain advantages, while the negative has succeeded in showing that certain disadvantages will also result. There is always the remote possibility that the judge, under these conditions, will decide that the disadvantages exactly balance the advantages, and he might be tempted to declare the debate a draw. Such a decision would be erroneous, for the affirmative has failed to establish reason for adopting the plan. Surely if a plan's defects exactly balance its merits, the plan offers no improvement. Therefore the decision must go to the negative.

As a second example, assume that the negative has offered a counterplan, and at the end of the debate it appears that both plans offer an improvement, but are of exactly equal merit. Even here the debate is not a tie. The negative, in offering a counterplan, said in effect, "The affirmative plan should not be adopted because it would interfere with the adoption of another, superior, plan—namely the one we are proposing." If, at the end of the debate, the negative has succeeded only in showing that its plan is of equal merit, it has failed to show that the affirmative's satisfactory remedy for the admittedly bad situation should not be adopted. Therefore the affirmative won.

As a third example, assume that all of the affirmative's alleged advantages were successfully refuted, while all of the negative's alleged disadvantages were also refuted. Under these circumstances, the judge might be tempted to declare a tie, but this would be incorrect; the proposed plan offers no improvement over the *status quo* and therefore should not be adopted. The negative must be given the decision.

In short, regardless of the position of the teams at the end of the debate, one or the other must be awarded the decision. There is no such thing as a tie in debating.

ANNOUNCING THE DECISION

The decision should always be announced immediately after the conclusion of the debate. Debaters like to know how the debate came out, win or lose, and there seems to be little point in delaying the announcement of the decision for several hours or even for a day or more, as is sometimes done. The judge should be expected to come to a conclusion within a few minutes after the debate; otherwise it will not be fresh in his mind and the wrong decision may result. Furthermore, the judge is in a position immediately after the debate to go over the two cases for the benefit of the teams, showing which arguments were satisfactorily answered and which were not. This is a valuable experience for debaters, coaches, and judge, and one which should not be needlessly sacrificed. In radio or television debates the judge usually comes to the microphone immediately after the last rebuttalist, announcing his decision and the reasons for it; this system has been found to work well and does not place too much of a burden on the judge.

It has often been said, in the case of decisions given orally by competent judges, that the decision was "the best part of the debate." This kind of remark is inspired by a judge only when he carefully analyzes the debate and explains to the teams and audience just why one team won.

A single critic judge should always give an oral criticism of the debate at the time he announces his decision unless specifically requested not to. A ten-minute summary of the arguments presented, showing which were answered and which were not, is one of his major duties. If he is using the double-summary technique, his critique will consist primarily of a review of his double-summary sheets.

Once the decision has been made and announced, the judge may make comments about the individual debaters. Here the judge is functioning more as a coach or counselor than as a judge, and remarks of this kind, while usually welcome, should be distinguished from the actual decision and the reasons for it. Sometimes comments about the individual debaters are reserved for a private conference after the audience has left in order to spare the feelings of the speakers. Unjust criticism or unjust praise should be avoided; most debaters prefer the judge to be completely objective in his comments.

It is desirable for the director of debate, when securing the judge, to mention that he is to give a critique of the debate. Not long ago a judge of doubtful ability, after telling one or two humorous stories, spent about fifteen minutes explaining how poor he thought the debate topic was for high school students, what he thought about the history and future of debate, and how well qualified he was to judge this particular contest because of his Ph.D. degree, his standing at one of the universities, and his work with Jan Christiaan Smuts (who incidentally was not mentioned in the debate). He then went on to say something about the good organization of the cases (which happened to be extremely poor) and concluded with, "All considered, I think the team from . . . won." The judge later explained to the coaches that he did not analyze the arguments because he had been hired to give a decision, not a critique. Incidents of this kind are unfortunate and are not likely to promote the confidence of the debaters in the judging.

Judges, as well as debaters, make use of strategy. Many judges, for instance, will announce the winning team only after the conclusion of their analyses of the debate. In this way, everyone concerned pays close attention to what they have to say.

A typical decision might sound something like this:

Thank you, Dr. Longwell. It is always a real pleasure to attend the Fall debate between these schools. I understand that the series is now in its twelfth year.

Fortunately, debate judges are not expected to know much about the debate topic. I am afraid that if I were to pose as an expert in tonight's company, I would quickly be exposed. You gentlemen have enlightened me considerably.

Of course, you are all interested in the outcome of the debate, so let us review briefly just what took place.

The affirmative presented two benefits, or advantages, for its plan.

First, the affirmative claimed that free trade, gradually accomplished over a twenty-year period through annual 5 per cent reductions, would materially improve our standard of living. In short, we would have more goods at a lower price. This is the classic argument for free trade, and the negative made little attempt to refute it. At the end of the debate it remained standing.

Second, the affirmative claimed that a free trade policy would help our foreign relations, particularly among countries friendly to us. The negative sharply disputed this, pointing out that many foreign countries have tariffs substantially higher than our own, and that it is not unreasonable to conclude that they are not much interested in free trade. The argument was tossed back and forth several times, including the questioning periods. I was not satisfied that it stood up under this barrage, and have marked it "not established."

So much for the affirmative case. Now let us examine the negative case.

The negative offered four defects or disadvantages in the free trade program, and concluded that we should retain our present tariff policy.

First, the negative claimed that a policy of free trade would produce unemployment, that low-priced foreign labor would throw our workers out of work. The negative pointed out that in this event, those who kept their jobs would pay higher taxes for the support of the unemployed. The affirmative replied that under free trade, each country would manufacture the goods it is best qualified to produce. Perhaps the Swiss would make most of the watch movements, but we would still assemble them here, and we would make other goods which would be shipped to Switzerland to pay for the watch movements. The affirmative further demonstrated through examples that tariffs can have as much effect as free trade in displacing workers from one job to another. The negative seemed to have no answer, and so this asserted defect or disadvantage was marked "not established."

Second, the negative claimed that free trade would lower farm incomes, that foreign nations would dump meat and grain at low prices. The affirmative replied that on the contrary, much of the prosperity of our farmers depends on exports, and that we cannot expect to export without importing. The affirmative concluded that free trade would help, not hurt, the farmer. The negative failed to reply.

Third, the negative claimed that free trade would weaken the United States militarily, that we would be forced to shut down industries that would be essential to us in time of war, such as tungsten mining. The affirmative replied that those industries would still be protected. The negative asked how they could be protected under a free trade policy, and where the affirmative would stop, since just about everything is essential in total war. The affirmative replied that for the most part, it was in favor of free trade, but that this did not preclude exceptions where clearly demonstrated to be essential. It indicated that such exceptions would be very rare, and that a board would investigate each individual case. The point was hotly contested, but the affirmative did seem to come out on top, so here again the defect or disadvantage was marked "not established."

Fourth, the negative protested that free trade would prevent the development of new industries, industries that could not survive world-wide competition for some time, but that might eventually if given a chance to get started without foreign competition. The affirmative quickly disposed of this by providing in its plan a twenty-year period of protection for infant industries, and quick elimination of tariffs after the end of the twenty years.

So, at the end of the debate, I find that the affirmative succeeded in making one advantage stick—free trade would bring us more goods at lower prices, raising our standard of living. The negative was not able to establish any disadvantage. The plan was demonstrated to be better than our present trade policy, the affirmative met its burden of proof, and therefore I award the decision to the affirmative.

Now for a few comments about the individual debaters. You understand, of course, that the remarks which follow are simply suggestions and observations to help you in the future, and have no part in the decision.

Mr. March, I think your first speech might have been more effective if you had given us more of an idea of what your plan would be expected to accomplish, and how. As it was, we had to wait for the second affirmative speech for this information. You did give us considerable background material, and you did make it quite clear that a problem of some kind does exist—"need," you called it—but it was not clear to me how you intended to improve matters. I was reminded of the politician who campaigned against sin. Everyone was against it, but that alone gave no reason to vote for him. Perhaps you were holding back on purpose, but at the end of your speech, I had no reason to believe that the affirmative had an improvement to offer. At least, you didn't tell me what it was, or how you would bring it about.

Mr. Cummings, your facts and organization were excellent, and you were especially strong in summary. I do feel, however, that I should call your attention to a rather bad habit, that of wiggling and twisting. Those things are distracting, of course. Now there's no penalty for wiggling, but it is quite possible that while I was busy watching you, I missed part of your train of thought. If so, you exacted your own penalty. I think probably you simply have stage fright. Why not practice in front of a mirror? You'll be surprised how much that can help. And, of course, the more practice debates in which you take part, the more at ease you'll be. I don't want to minimize the fine presentation you made, and I do feel that with practice you will turn out to be a very difficult opponent to meet.

Mr. Bemelman, your greatest strength was your platform presence. It is remarkably easy to follow a talk as effectively delivered as yours was.

Mr. Stahlings, your evidence and organization were excellent. It was an impressive job, and I am sure it helped your team considerably.

That is all I have to say, gentlemen. It has been a pleasure to be with you tonight, and I wish both teams success for the remainder of the season.

Occasionally a judge, through foolish remarks made in his discussion of the debate, alienates forever the affections of those who hear his decision. Statements that a judge should not make include:

1. The affirmative presented a stronger and better organized case but used its notes too much, so I award the decision to the negative.

If the affirmative did a better job of debating, it should get the decision. The excessive use of notes may prevent a team (the affirmative in this case) from getting its ideas across to the judge, and as a result, it may very well lose the debate. However, in the above instance the use of notes presumably did not prevent the team from getting its ideas across. Therefore, the judge was wrong in giving the decision to the negative.

> 2. The negative presented a better case than the affirmative, but I am giving the decision to the affirmative because the negative failed to make use of certain arguments that, in my opinion, are very important and would have made the negative case much stronger.

The judge has no right to dictate to the teams which arguments they should have used. Certain arguments that appear good to the judge may deliberately be omitted because one team knows the opposition has a strong answer. Of course, if a team fails to refute a major argument of the opposition, the judge not only may, but must, consider this; but he may not penalize a team for omitting certain specific arguments that he may have in mind.

For instance, an affirmative team debating the federal world union question may, if it desires, claim that the union would curb soil erosion, that it would eliminate sickness, that it would aid materially in the reforestation of the Pacific coast, and that it would balance the budget of Buckingham County, Indiana. The judge must not penalize the team because it failed to mention the elimination of war; the benefits to be alleged for a plan are to be decided by the person doing the alleging. The same thing holds true with regard to the defects of a plan. The judge must judge on the basis of the arguments presented, not on the basis of arguments that might have been presented.

> 3. I think the affirmative is right. Therefore my decision goes to the affirmative.

The problem of which side is "right" is entirely irrelevant. The judge is judging a debate, not enacting legislation.

4. The negative case was stronger than the affirmative, but the decision goes to the affirmative because the negative side was easier to defend, and considering the material available, the affirmative did a better job.

The judge is not in a position to decide which side of a resolution is easier, because of the very large (one is tempted to say "infinite") number of cases possible. Sometimes the subject appears one-sided because one team was shrewd enough to think up an unusual approach giving it an advantage. This is to the credit of that team; to penalize it would be to reward the lack of ingenuity of the other team.

It should also be recognized that the "easier" side of a debate topic may vary throughout the year, showing that neither side actually is easier, but only apparently so. The natural conclusion is that if the debaters actually were seriously handicapped on one side of the topic, they would not change their minds so often about which side of the topic this is. Baccus [2] remarks:

What happens after debate? After ten years of experience I differ from the critics of debate as to what happens then. It may be the case of one man's word against another. I present the following experience as logical and reasonable. It has happened this way practically every year.

First the debaters study the question, and immediately there is a superficial judgment that one side is easier or harder, more nearly right than the other. Then there is an investigation of material and invariably within three weeks a change of mind takes place, so that the other side is now considered the stronger. Then, as he is able to present his views on the platform before opponents who had been thinking along different lines, the debater changes his mind again, believing as originally, but with the significant difference that there are more logical reasons for believing as he now does. As the season continues the shifts back and forth continue, one side being considered stronger than the other, then the reverse, now the affirmative, now the negative, now because of this reason, now because of that combination of arguments or points of view. . . . The final product is belief, conviction, sometimes moral judgment for the debater.

[2] Joseph H. Baccus, "Unique Values of Competitive Debate," *Forensic*, 23: 81, March 1938.

This happens only because standard debating topics are remarkably well balanced and because their full depths are seldom if ever probed by the speakers. In other words the judge, even if he is a debate coach, is in no position to state definitely that one side is easier than the other, and therefore he should make no effort to compensate for any apparent unevenness in the topic.

5. The affirmative did a better job of debating until the rebuttal, but my decision goes to the negative because the affirmative spent its entire rebuttal on summary instead of refutation. If the affirmative had spent any time on refutation in the rebuttal period, I would have given the decision to the affirmative.

This judge does not understand debating. If a rebuttalist can show that his own team's major arguments remain standing while those of the opposition have not been established, he is accomplishing his major function; once this is done, he should sit down, for the debate has been won.

While the five remarks quoted above are all of the type that cause coaches to leave debates muttering under their breath, all five have been heard in intercollegiate debates.

Problems of this kind are not new. Potter[3] quotes from an 1899 decision:

The judges stated that the debate was very close. They said the mass of evidence brought forward by Columbia showed the Chicago side to be intrinsically so weak, that they would give the decision to Chicago because of the difficulty of her task.

Surely no comment is necessary.

JUDGE'S BALLOT

The typical judge's ballot looks something like the one on page 114. A nice gesture is for the host to fill out the top portion before it is handed to the judge.

[3] David Potter, ed., *Argumentation and Debate* (New York, Dryden Press, 1954), p. 15.

Judge's Ballot

TOPIC

....

....

PARTICIPANTS

Affirmative—school: ....

  Speakers: ....

....

Negative—school: ....

  Speakers: ....

....

DECISION

In my opinion, the better debating was done by the .... side, and therefore I award the decision to that team.

(Signed) ...., Judge

Score Sheet *versus* Double Summary

Since two methods of judging are recognized and available, there will probably always be some who will prefer one to the other. One method requires the judge to assign points to various elements of effective debating; the other method requires the judge to follow the arguments and refutation.

The two methods may be contrasted as follows:

Score sheet method

Advantages

1. The system is easy to learn. Just about anyone can say, "I think I'll give that man 3 on reasoning."
2. It gives the judge some idea of relative strengths, at least more of an idea than he would have without some system.

Disadvantages

1. The decision may go to the wrong team. Too much reliance is placed on arbitrary lists and points with little meaning.
2. No consideration is given to the fact that some elements may be more important than others in a given debate.
3. It is undesirable to teach debaters to emphasize elements for their own sake, when they should be looked upon as incidental means to an end.

Double summary method

Advantage

It gives an objective answer, based on accomplishment.

Disadvantage

It requires a judge who knows his job, and who is alert.

7

ADMINISTRATION

There is a surprisingly close parallel between directing a successful sales program and a successful forensic program. In either case, recruiting, training, and stimulation of participants play an important part.

RECRUITING

New members of the high school or college debate squad are recruited by (1) personal solicitation, (2) advertising in one form or another, and (3) group meetings.

Personal solicitation has long been one of the most effective recruiting methods. Promising debaters are "spotted" by present members of the squad or by cooperative teachers. Squad members then talk to these prospects and persuade them to come out for debate.

Advertising may take the form of posters in the halls, articles in the school paper, announcements in assemblies, or, if the school has its own radio station, announcements over the radio.

Group meetings are often held for this purpose, particularly in college. The event should be well advertised in advance. Cider and doughnuts, and an air of informality, may be the order of the day. Old members mix with the prospects. The president or manager may tell what he enjoys about debate, and what he gets out of it. He may also tell something about the schedule of events for the coming year. Following the talk, a short debate may be held on a humorous topic. The prospects are usually asked to sign up then and there, perhaps on individual forms passed out for this purpose. The forms can be designed so that everyone has some writing to do, whether he is coming out for debate or not.

An indirect method of recruiting is through intramural debates, held in the English classes. English teachers are usually happy to cooperate because of the educational values. The debate organization should be prepared to furnish the chairman, timekeeper, and some coaching. The debates can be judged by the class. The decision may not mean much, but the point is to get everyone interested. Oregon style is, of course, very desirable in this situation. An outright request or suggestion to the English students that they come out for the regular debate squad would be inappropriate, but the result is still achieved: The interest of the English students is stimulated, and some promising prospects are located for subsequent personal solicitation.

It is a mistake to try to be too selective in recruiting. Some will apply who will never be able to make the varsity, but a well-rounded program will include intrasquad debates, and such individuals can still be given their chance. Furthermore, some very unpromising prospects turn out to be good debaters when given the chance. Who is to say that they should not be allowed to compete on a fair-and-square basis?

Finally, it should be recognized that in order to secure a top-notch varsity, it is necessary to have a substantially larger number of squad members. The debate director should put the law of averages to work for him. If he obtains 50 recruits per year, he has twice as good a chance to find those few top-notch men as does the director who recruits only 25. He need not worry about having too many to handle. The hopelessly unfit will soon drop out, and a local program can keep the others active and useful.

TRAINING RECRUITS

Every coach has some kind of training program. Group meetings, coaching of individual teams, and practice debates all play a part.

The coach has two groups to deal with—the recruits and the experienced debaters. For the most part, they present separate problems: the newcomers have to learn how to debate; the old-timers have to learn the new topic, and how to debate better.

The practice debate is one of the most popular and effective devices for training recruits. It has been asserted that a team does not begin to debate until it has engaged in some fifty contests. Whatever the figure, it is clear that there is no substitute for experience.

The practice debates can begin quickly after the squad has been gathered in the fall. Most of the recruits have probably never heard a debate, but that makes little difference. They can be given literature to read and told to prepare for the first practice debate, which may be two weeks away. There may be too many recruits at this stage for each team to receive extensive personal coaching before the first practice debate, but help can be given in the fundamentals and in debate procedure. Varsity members may help, through a "buddy" program.

When the recruits take part in their first practice debates, the results are usually rough, but that is to be expected. The important thing is that they now know what a debate is; the ground has been prepared for some real work.

Second, third, and fourth rounds may quickly follow the first, perhaps at one-week intervals. During this period the recruits learn how to find and organize material, and how to meet opposing arguments.

A rigorous schedule of practice debates has one other effect: Some of the recruits find that debate requires too much work, or is over their heads, and drop out. As the group narrows, the amount of individual coaching will, of course, increase.

After some five or six weeks, some of the recruits may be ready to try some outside contests. Contract debates and novice tournaments are ideal for this purpose. During these early debates, coventional cases are almost always presented, without any surprises in evidence or case structure. This is partly because the recruits are not ready for anything else, and partly because they do not want to put the opposition on guard.

Practice debates generally taper off after the outside contests begin, but may continue on a less frequent schedule all season.

Another excellent training device is the squad meeting. Meetings may be called to discuss common problems, or to practice refutation or cross-examination, or to hear varsity debaters compete against each other.

Meetings should start and end on time. It is easy to kill student interest by calling meetings for (say) 7 o'clock and then starting them at 7:20. No one likes to sit around waiting for others to show up. If the meeting doesn't start on time, it won't be considered necessary to come on time to the next one either. And once that habit is established, it is hard to break. The director has the responsibility for starting the meeting at the scheduled hour, even if only one student is present. The others will respect him for it, and are more likely to come on time in the future.

Absenteeism at meetings should be kept to a minimum. One director who secured very nearly 100 per cent attendance at evening meetings throughout the year had a very simple but effective system. He always scheduled meetings several weeks in advance and insisted that anyone who could not attend notify him *in advance* of the meeting. Then, when the group assembled he explained to the others why that individual could not attend.

Training the Varsity

In the early days of intercollegiate debating in this country, each college scheduled two or three debates a year, seldom more than half a dozen. This made it possible to concentrate an extraordinary effort on each debate, which not infrequently included several months of preparation. Today schedules of fifty to seventy-five intercollegiate debates a year are not uncommon, and a shorter schedule of preparation has become inevitable. Only by participating in debate tournaments, by regularly using the annual national question in contract debates, and by maintaining a relatively large debate squad, have schools been able to carry schedules of this magnitude without sacrificing quality. At present about six weeks of preparation can often be devoted to a tournament or series of contract debates. A suggested six-week schedule of preparation follows:

First week:

1. Reading material relevant to the topic
2. Considering possible plans and counterplans
3. Considering the possible advantages and disadvantages that can be ascribed to these plans in the debates
4. Gathering material to support the arguments on both sides
5. Deciding upon a tentative case
6. Outlining the tentative case in writing and turning it in to the coach
7. Delivering the constructive speeches to the coach

[A great deal of inertia must be overcome by the coach when preparation for a debate series is begun. Unless he insists on a stiff schedule for the first week, and unless he requires the debaters to write their outlines and deliver their speeches to him, he often finds that the result is procrastination rather than action.

Coaches who find, when the speeches are delivered, that the debaters lack poise and confidence, should have them deliver their talks over and over again until this confidence has been gained. The repetition of a short speech twenty or twenty-five times will do wonders in improving delivery and will convince the debater that he should practice in the same way at home in the future.]

Second week:

1. Considering unexpected approaches that might be used in both the plan and counterplan
2. Investigating the strength of arguments that might be used to support these cases
3. Revising the case if necessary
4. Delivering to the coach the revised speeches on the side of the topic that will be upheld in the tournament
5. Practicing the oral refutation of arguments presented by the coach
6. Taking part in at least one practice debate

Third week:

1. Engaging in at least two practice debates on the side of the topic that will be upheld in the tournament
2. Devising answers to new arguments of opponents, and answers to the answers, and answers to those answers
3. Gathering material to support these rebuttal arguments

[At least two teams should be assigned for each tournament, even though only one team will actually participate. When a tournament calls for two teams from each school it is wise to go even farther by having four teams (two affirmative and two negative) prepare for the contests. This furnishes material for practice debates and brings out several different viewpoints. It also enables the coach to delay his selection of the final teams until the last week before the tournament, thus encouraging hard work on the part of all of the debaters.[1]]

Fourth week:

1. Engaging in three practice debates, including one on the opposite side of the topic
2. Revising the case where necessary, even to the extent of working out an entirely new case
3. Strengthening the evidence supporting the claimed advantages and disadvantages

Fifth week:

1. Engaging in two or more practice debates, including one on each side of the topic
2. Revising the case as required
3. Strengthening the evidence supporting the advantages and disadvantages of both the affirmative and negative plans
4. Selecting the teams to take part in the tournament

[This last action should always be taken by the coach. Selection of the teams by an advisory committee cannot be recommended.]

Sixth week:

1. Deciding upon the case to be used
2. Providing an alternate case for use if the first case is found unsuccessful, or for use if the first case is based on surprise and becomes known
3. Engaging in two or three practice debates, all on the side to be presented in the tournament

[The teams should be willing to revise their cases right up to the last minute. On one occasion a debater devised an exceptionally good strategic case while the men were on their way to the tournament; the team dropped its previous plans, worked out the strategic case, and defeated all opposition in the tournament.]

[1] Carroll P. Lahman, in his *Debate Coaching* (New York, H. W. Wilson Company, 1936), p. 125, says, "The whole squad should be kept on its toes, working for a place on the team, and that can't be done if you announce a month in advance that A, B, and C will constitute the team. A let-down in the efforts of the other squad members is inevitable, even though later debates are on the schedule."

The above schedule is not inflexible; it must be modified to suit the conditions under which each individual school works. There is no substitute for practice debating, however, and whatever schedule of preparation is used, emphasis on the practice debate must remain.

STIMULATION

Hard work on the part of students can be stimulated by various forms of recognition. Membership in an honor society is an award that some students strongly desire. Others respond to recognition at banquets, newspaper stories, pins, trophies, and other awards.

There should be one top award in every program, something so difficult to attain that only a handful of the very best debaters can receive it. It does not make much difference what the award is. The important thing is the achievement it represents, and the public recognition that goes with it. The award need not be costly; a distinctive lapel pin or key might be appropriate.

Careful thought should be given to the qualifications for the top award. Surely it will have to be based on successful debating, however that is measured. No sales manager gives much recognition to the salesman who fails to convince his customers to buy. Trying hard isn't enough. Good intentions aren't enough. A salesman is expected to sell. And the top debater is expected to win. If he fails to close his "sale" to the audience and judge, that contest should not be credited toward the top award. Or, if it is credited, then less credit should be given for a loss than for a win.

There is also considerable satisfaction in a word of praise. A quiet, "Well done," from the coach can be a powerful incentive to the debater.

Best efforts are put forth by debaters who are properly stimulated in a competitive atmosphere. This training will serve them well in the years that follow graduation.

Publicity

Publicity for the debate program can be developed in several ways. One of the best is to hold exhibition debates. Kiwanis and Rotary clubs, school classes, and church groups furnish ready-made audiences. Special audiences can be attracted with the right sales approach, if the product is good.

It is well, when planning audience debates, to choose a topic of intense interest to the people who are likely to come. The national topic is not good for this purpose. Some burning campus issue is better, or a political topic in election year.

The next step is to make sure everyone knows about the coming event. Articles can be written for the school newspaper and the city newspaper. Local radio and television news broadcasters can be informed. Posters can be placed. Direct mail can be used. Suppose, for instance, that the topic chosen is of especial interest to lawyers. The classified section of the telephone book will give the names and addresses of the city's lawyers. An interesting direct mail piece (not too commercial—more like a personal letter) can be very effective in securing an audience. Teachers can be invited in person, as well as by mail.

Newspaper stories can be written at about weekly intervals when there is an active program. Names and pictures of winners can appear, and human interest stories can be written about unusual happenings.

All of these things promote general interest in the debate program; once started in the right direction, interest mushrooms.

Staff Organization

A full-scale debate program is too much for the coach to handle, unless he has more time than most. A common solution is to appoint a student debate manager, who handles the correspondence and much of the detail.

Large programs go far beyond this point. Some college squads utilize thirty or more squad members in various assignments. Sometimes not all of them are debaters. The purpose is two-fold: to get the work done, and to encourage the newcomers to work for a top job through a self-perpetuating student organization. A student organization of this kind can turn out a substantial amount of work, but it can also be over-organized and sluggish, especially if the top men are not on the job as they should be.

One organization of this kind is tabulated below. The freshmen are assigned to the menial jobs, of course. The sophomores hold the next level, then the juniors, and then the seniors. Each year, as the seniors leave, the hardest-working juniors are promoted and others dropped. The hardest-working sophomores are promoted to the junior level, and others dropped. The most promising freshmen are promoted to the sophomore level, and others dropped. "Dropped," of course, does not mean dropped from debate; it simply means that the lazy or less competent ones are dropped from the staff organization. The decisions are made each year by the outgoing seniors. The organization looks something like this:

President and General Manager (senior)
   Debate Manager (senior)
      Tournament Manager (junior)
         Assistant Tournament Managers (sophomores)
      Radio-TV Debate Manager (junior)
         Assistant Radio-TV Debate Managers (sophomores)
      Contract Debate Manager (junior)
         Assistant Contract Debate Managers (sophomores)
      Squad Debate Manager (junior)
         Assistant Squad Debate Managers (sophomores)
   Activities Director (senior)
      Forum Director (junior)
         Assistant Forum Directors (sophomores)
      Publicity Director (junior)
         Assistant Publicity Directors (sophomores)
      Librarian (sophomore)
   Treasurer (senior)
      Assistant Treasurers (juniors)

RAISING MONEY

Every debate group needs a source of funds. On the college level, this may take the form of an appropriation from the activities fund, perhaps supplemented by plays or other money-raising activities. Budgets for colleges range from $25 to $5000 per year, though most schools are grouped in the $600 to $1200 range, according to a 1950 survey.[2]

On the high school level, less money is needed and all of it may be raised by students. National Forensic League members are currently raising funds in many ways.[3] They reported these activities, among others:

> Car washing; variety shows, in which speech, drama, and music groups combine; showing of movies during study periods and lunch hour; sponsorship of famous speakers; typing and mimeograph work; sale of popcorn, soft drinks, candy and cowbells at football games; sale of ballpoint pens, Christmas cards and greeting cards; operation of a hot chocolate dispensing machine in the hall; and sponsorship of dances and roller skating parties.

Obtaining Judges

Debate judging requires men who have other qualifications than a high standing in the community. It makes little difference whether the judge is an expert or a complete stranger to the subject being debated, as long as he understands how to judge and as long as he remains impartial.

In tournament debating, the visiting coaches are usually asked to judge. They are assigned, of course, to debates in which their own teams are not participating.

In contract debating, the problem is a little harder to solve, particularly if there are not very many qualified men in the area.

Some of the best judging is done by active debate coaches and by former debaters. These men and women know debate.

Many schools have been successful using lawyers as judges; this is because lawyers, by training, understand how to keep track of arguments presented, their refutation and counter-refutation. There are several important differences between debate procedure and courtroom procedure, particularly in regard to evidence, and if the judge is a lawyer, he

[2] David, Potter, ed., *Argumentation and Debate* (New York, Dryden Press, 1954), p. 364.

[3] *Rostrum*, 30:9-10, November 1955.

needs to know these differences. Clergymen lean a little too strongly toward emotional appeals to make good judges, although of course there are exceptions. Teachers of speech sometimes make competent judges after they have had debating experience, but too often they pay more attention to enunciation and gestures than to what the speakers are saying, and too frequently their training makes it difficult for them to understand the basic judging procedure which ignores such items except as means to an end. Regardless of the profession of the judge, the one essential qualification is that he understand how to judge debates; this should be self-evident, but it is surprising how many times judges are picked for other qualifications.

It is usually desirable, when a series of debates is to be held, to systematize the procedure for obtaining judges. Many colleges use this plan: The debate management keeps a card index of all judges who have been used in the past, together with their addresses, telephone numbers, qualifications, and experience in judging for that school. The less experienced judges are used for subvarsity debates, while the better judges are asked to decide the varsity meets. Each judge is asked to recommend others, so that the list is constantly enlarged. A new judge is tried first on a subvarsity debate, and if his comments at the end show that he knows how to judge, he is promoted to the varsity. The working list of judges is kept as large as possible. Debates are scheduled well in advance so that if the judge refuses for some particular date, he can be invited at once for some other debate later in the year. In this way, a competent judge can almost always be found without difficulty.

It is also a good idea, even when using experienced judges, to mail each one a pamphlet or series of mimeographed sheets explaining the rules of debate and the principles of judging. A debate judge needs to know the rules of debate just as a basketball referee needs to know the rules of basketball, and it is difficult to see how he can learn these rules unless someone sends a copy to him.

Some schools make a practice of paying a fee to the judge, and this practice is to be commended if the necessary funds can be raised. If a fee (say ten dollars) is to be paid, care should be taken to mention at the time the judge is invited that the customary fee of . . . dollars will be tendered. This tells the judge how much he will get and also lets him know that it is a judging fee, not a bribe. It seems true that where a fee is paid, the quality of the judging is higher, not only because the best men can be obtained more frequently, but because the judge puts more thought and effort into his study of the rules of debate and into his judging.

The financial difficulties involved in raising the money for this fee are particularly acute in the case of small schools with heavy schedules. A ten dollar fee paid for each of fifty debates is five hundred dollars, and there are some schools which consider fifty debates in one year a relatively light schedule. In spite of this cost, the fact remains that the judging fee has become more and more common. The financial difficulties are being overcome. One method is the use of neutral coaches, without fee, as the judges of tournaments, thus reducing the number of debates for which outside judges must be hired, and at the same time permitting heavy schedules to be arranged each year. In many sections of the country all judges except neutral coaches are now paid a fee, and the remaining localities must adopt this practice if they intend to secure competent judging.

To summarize, three practices are to be recommended as ways of insuring competent decisions. If maximum results are to be obtained, all three must be followed simultaneously and consistently.

1. A systematic procedure should be followed in recording the names and qualifications of judges.

2. Each judge should be furnished with a copy of the rules of debate and an explanation of the correct judging procedure. This material should be sent far enough in advance for him to study before the debate.

3. If financially possible, a regular fee should be paid.

Forms

Records, in any kind of business, are kept for two purposes: current operating information and historical reference. Printed forms are great time-savers if properly designed. They should be few in number, and simple. They should show every bit of necessary information, and nothing else. Complex or inadequate records are of little use.

Forms are best designed by persons who are familiar with the work to be performed, who understand printing, and who have an eye for layout. It is a mistake to assume that anyone can design a good form.

The records required by the director of debate will vary with the size and type of debate programs. In the chapter on judging, the double-summary sheets and the judge's ballot are illustrated. In addition, the director of an active group may well use these forms:

1. Debate contract
   When debating individual schools, it is well to rely on written contracts to avoid any possible misunderstanding about the arrangements.

2. Debate record
   This is a basic record, giving the details of each past debate. Information appearing on it can later be broken down in various ways by clerical help if desired.
   One of the most important uses of the debate record is to compile the participation record of each debater.

3. Participation record
   A sheet is prepared for each member of the squad, showing his background and his debating record.
   This file is particularly useful in distributing assignments and awards fairly. It also serves as a valuable historical record of past debaters.

4. Judge record
   A record of judges is maintained, one sheet for each, showing qualifications and experience in judging for this school.
   Schools relying on contract, rather than tournament, debating need to have as many judges in mind as can possibly be mustered.
   Information regarding the judge's background may be as extensive as desired, but it is considered unethical to show which way the judge voted, because someone might be tempted to pick judges who in the past have voted a certain way.

Two major files will be required, other than files of the above records. They are:

1. Correspondence file
   Correspondence is ordinarily filed by school. Included are current contracts and current letters, as well as items of particular historical interest from preceding seasons.
2. Transcripts and outlines of past debates. This type of material is ordinarily filed by topic.

CONTRACT FOR DEBATE

PARTICIPATING SCHOOLS

.... and
....

GENERAL PROVISIONS

Date: ...., 19...... Time: ....
Place: ....
Classification: ( ) Varsity   ( ) Freshman
The host will provide overnight lodging and meals for out-of-town visitors: .... men and .... women.
Platform furnishings, audience, selection of judge, timekeeping, and similar details will be arranged by the host.
On arrival, visitors should report to: ....

TOPIC

( ) Current national college topic. Subject: ....
( ) Current national high school topic. Subject: ....
Full wording (if other): ....
....
....
Definitions agreed upon are recorded on the back of this form.
The affirmative side will be taken by: ....

TIMING

Debaters per team: ( ) two   ( ) three
Constructive speeches: ...... per team, of ...... minutes each
Questioning periods: ...... per team, of ...... minutes each
Rebuttal speeches: ...... per team, of ...... minutes each

DECISION

( ) Critic judge   ( ) Audience shift-of-opinion   ( ) None
Other: ....

APPROVED

....
By ....   By ....

RECORD OF DEBATE

Opponent: ....
Date: .... Classification: ( ) varsity
( ) freshman

Topic: ( ) Current national topic
Full wording (if other) ....
....
....

Side: ( ) Affirmative
( ) Negative

Debaters on our team: ....
....
....

Style: ( ) Standard 10-5
( ) Oregon 8-5-8
If other, specify ....
....

Decision: ( ) Won ( ) Lost ( ) No decision
Name of judge: ....
Coach's comments: ....

PARTICIPATION RECORD

Debater's name: ....
Course and class: ....
Scholastic work in debate and related fields: ....
....
Experience before coming to this school: ....
....

PARTICIPATION

Date	Opponent	Result		
		Won	Lost	No Dec.

AWARDS
....
....
....

JUDGE RECORD

Name of judge: ....
                        Last   Title   First   Middle

Home address: ....

Home telephone: ....

Office address: ....

Office telephone: ....

QUALIFICATIONS

  Occupation: ....

  Ever debated?   ( ) yes   ( ) no

  Ever coached?   ( ) yes   ( ) no

  Member forensic honor society: Which? ....

  Comments re ability: ....

  ....

  ....

  Possible bias: Previously connected with the following schools:

....

EXPERIENCE JUDGING FOR US

Dates only:

EXTENT AND VALUES OF DEBATE TODAY

Extent

Debate today is a widespread activity. While there is no official tabulation, it appears from published reports that each year there are some fifty to one hundred high school tournaments, plus an undetermined number of individual contract debates. High school tournaments are sponsored by (1) the National University Extension Association's state leagues, (2) the National Forensic League, and (3) individual colleges for high schools in their vicinities.

The South St. Paul (Minnesota) High School reported in March 1955, that it had a season's record of 326 wins and 59 losses.[1] On about the same date the Hutchinson (Kansas) High School reported that it had won 256 debates for the year, placing second in the state. The Pittsburgh (Kansas) High School reported winning 258 debates in one recent season.

College activity seems to be running at about the same level. There appear to be about the same number of intercollegiate tournaments, plus an undetermined number of individual contract debates.

Organizations

College level:

Delta Sigma Rho	79 chapters, with considerable strength among the state universities
Pi Kappa Delta	174 chapters, mostly among smaller schools, many of which have strong and active debate programs

[1] *Rostrum,* 19:9, March 1955.

Tau Kappa Alpha	93 chapters, with stress on scholarship as well as forensic ability

Because of the similarity of their goals, proposals for the merger of two or more have been advanced and are currently under discussion.

Junior college level:

Phi Rho Pi	The chapter list is not published, but the current active group is believed to number about 75. Hard hit by the war, the organization is now staging a come-back.

High school level:

National Forensic League	Approximately 700 chapters in high schools with particularly strong forensic programs.
NUEA state leagues	Organizations for the sponsorship of state tournaments and distribution of literature.

Professional groups:

American Forensic Association	The professional organization for coaches and forensic directors; a vigorous newcomer to the scene.
Speech Association of America	The professional organization in the more general field of speech.

DEBATING IN OTHER COUNTRIES

Intercollegiate debates have been held with teams from several countries, including England, Scotland, Germany, Australia, Hawaii, and, of course, Canada. Sometimes these teams visit the United States, sometimes American teams travel abroad.

There has been considerable progress in the Philippines in recent years, as evidenced by the writing and publishing of a full-length debate text for Philippine debaters.

The story of Japanese debating is especially interesting. Debating was brought to Japan by two former students of the University of Southern California, Messrs. Kanchi and Itabashi. These young men had not debated themselves, but had observed closely. They felt that they could serve their country well by bringing debate to it, and so they did.

Mr. Kanchi has written a text book in Japanese and has translated other material. He helped start Japanese-language debates in 1946. He reports that Japanese-language debate is now in fashion among the student and non-student youngsters of almost every prefecture.

Mr. Kanchi has also organized Japanese language debates among the prisoners at Yokohama Prison, and reports that lawyers, professors and high prison officials were astonished at the enthusiasm displayed and the excellence of reasoning power.

English-language intercollegiate contests began in Japan in 1950. They appear to be organized in the manner of our tournaments, although spread over a longer period of time. The winners have been:

    1950 St. Paul's University
    1951 Hitotsubashi University
    1952 Tokyo University
    1953 St. Paul's University
    1954 Tokyo University of Foreign Studies

The contests are sponsored by the International Education Center and *Asahi Shimbun*, Tokyo's largest newspaper. An attractive printed program is prepared for the final contest, which is held at Asahi Auditorium. Supporters listed on the program are the Ministry of Foreign Affairs, the Ministry of Education, *Nippon Times*, *Asahi Evening News*, the Japan Office of the *Reader's Digest*, and the International Students' Association of Japan.

The rules appearing in COMPETITIVE DEBATE are the standard debating rules of Japan. This book is used as the English-language text, and mimeographed copies of the rules are distributed without charge. Debates are held in Oregon style.

Professor Egbert Ray Nichols, formerly head of the Speech Department at the University of Redlands, recently spent some time in Japan lecturing students on debate.

The Japanese debaters have not yet met an American **team.**

VALUES

The long-range values of debate have been mentioned many times: learning to think on one's feet, learning how to find and organize material, learning how to talk. Such talents seem correlated with responsible positions after graduation, as evidenced by the number listed in *Who's Who.* Ewbank,[2] for instance, reports that 11 per cent of the Delta Sigma Rho members who graduated before 1928 are listed in *Who's Who in America.* Former debaters hold prominent positions in almost every walk of life, up to and including the United States Supreme Court bench and the vice presidency of the United States.

A list[3] of some familiar names among former debaters includes:

> Berle, Adolf A. (former Assistant Secretary of State)
>   DSR, Harvard University
> Best, George L. (Vice President, American Telephone and Telegraph Company)
>   TKA, University of Vermont
> Blankingship, Alexander H. (Bishop, Protestant Episcopal Church) TKA, University of Richmond
> Brashares, Charles W. (Bishop, Methodist Church)
>   DSR, Ohio Wesleyan College

[2] Henry Lee Ewbank, "What's Right with Debate," *Quarterly Journal of Speech,* 37:197-202, April 1951.

[3] Principle sources of information are "The Delta Sigma Rho Golden Jubilee Assembly," by E. C. Buehler, *Gavel,* 38:5-25, November 1955; "Alumni of Tau Kappa Alpha Hold Prominent Positions Throughout the Nation," *Speaker,* 33:2:1-12, January 1951; and *Who's Who in America.* It has not been learned whether or not any of the affiliations listed are honorary. In some cases the student's active participation in debate may have taken place at a school other than the one from which he was graduated.

Bricker, John W. (U.S. Senator)
DSR, Ohio State University
Bullitt, William C. (former Ambassador to Russia and France)
DSR, Ohio State University
Canham, Erwin D. (Editor, *Christian Science Monitor*)
DSR, Bates College
Clapp, Gordon R. (former Chairman, Tennessee Valley Author-
ity)
TKA, Lawrence College
Clark, Bennett Champ (former U.S. Senator)
DSR, University of Missouri
Coe, Conway P. (Vice President, Radio Corporation of America)
TKA, Randolph-Macon College
Corson, Fred B. (Bishop, Methodist Church; President, Dickin-
son College)
TKA, Dickinson College
Douglas, William O. (Justice, U.S. Supreme Court)
DSR, Whitman College
DuBridge, Lee A. (President, California Institute of Technology)
TKA, Cornell College
Edwards, Morris (President, Cincinnati Street Railway Company)
TKA, Wabash College
Graham, Frank P. (President, University of North Carolina)
TKA, University of North Carolina
Humphrey, Hubert H. (U.S. Senator)
NFL; DSR, University of Minnesota
Hutchins, Robert M. (Director, Fund for the Republic; former
Chancellor, University of Chicago)
DSR ,Yale University
Johnson, Lyndon B. (U.S. Senate Majority Leader)
Southwest Texas State Teachers College
Kaltenborn, Hans V. (radio commentator)
DSR, Harvard University
Lee, Joshua (Member, Civil Aeronautics Board; former U.S.
Senator)
DSR, University of Oklahoma
Lilienthal, David E. (former Chairman, Tennessee Valley
Authority and Atomic Energy Commission)
DSR, DePauw University
Lord, John W. (Bishop, Methodist Church)
TKA, Dickinson College
Long, Russell B. (U.S. Senator)
TKA, Louisiana State University
Luce, Henry R. (Editor and Publisher of *Time*)
DSR, Yale University
Malott, Deane Waldo (President, Cornell University)
DSR, University of Kansas

Martin, Paul E. (Bishop, Methodist Church)
TKA, Southern Methodist University

McNutt, Paul V. (Governor of Indiana, 1933-37; High Commissioner to the Philippine Islands, 1937-39, 1945-46; Chairman, War Manpower Commission, 1942-45)

Morse, Wayne (U.S. Senator)
DSR, University of Wisconsin

Monroney, Mike (U.S. Senator)
NFL, Central High School, Oklahoma City

Mundt, Karl E. (U.S. Senator)
NFL co-founder and national president; DSR, PKD, TKA, Carlton College; debate coach, Teachers' College, Madison, S.D.

Nixon, Richard (Vice President)
Whittier College

O'Connor, Basil (Chairman, National Foundation for Infantile Paralysis)
DSR, Dartmouth University

Oxnam, G. Bromley (Bishop, Methodist Church)
DSR, University of Southern California

Pearson, Drew (newspaper columnist)
DSR, Swarthmore College

Price, Byron (Assistant General Secretary, United Nations; former Director of Censorship)
TKA, Wabash College

Reed, Marshall R. (Bishop, Methodist Church)
DSR, Albion College

Romulo, Carlos P. (General; former aide-de-camp to General MacArthur)
TKA, University of Philippines

Rutledge, Wiley E. (Justice, U.S. Supreme Court, 1943-49)
DSR, University of Wisconsin

Ryan, Oswald (former Chairman, Civil Aeronautics Board)
TKA, Butler College; co-founder of TKA

Smith, W. Angie (Bishop, Methodist Church)
TKA, Southwestern University

Stassen, Harold E. (former Governor of Minnesota; former President of the University of Pennsylvania; Special Assistant to the President, to direct studies of disarmament)
DSR, University of Minnesota

Thomas, Lowell (radio commentator)
TKA, University of Denver

Willkie, Wendell (candidate for President, 1940)
Elwood High School, Indiana; DSR, University of Indiana

While it is true that debate does seem to help men get ahead, the debater does not have to wait until graduation to begin reaping the rewards of debate preparation. At least three benefits come to him while he is still in school.

The first and most obvious benefit is personal enjoyment. A debater likes competitive debate. It's fun. Once he has taken part, once he has felt the thrill of matching wits with his opponents before an audience, no great sales effort is necessary to keep him interested.

The second immediate return to the debater is his school work. Various studies have indicated that debaters get better-than-average grades. This, of course, doesn't necessarily mean that debate is responsible. Quite possibly both the high marks and the participation in debate were brought about by a different cause—a high IQ.

Nevertheless, debating does sometimes help in classroom work. One student took an economics examination which involved both cartels and the Keynes Plan, subjects he had debated earlier in the year. He attributes his A in that course at least in part to the impression made by his examination paper, which in turn could be attributed to debate.

In another case, two students who had been debating the tariff problem happened to be in the same class. The problem was mentioned in the text, and the instructor ventured a mild opinion, whereupon the two students jumped on it with both feet, showing all the arguments on the other side. When the discussion became embarrassingly one-sided, the debaters proceeded to change sides and show the arguments on the other side. They attributed their A's at least in part to the showing made that day.

The connection between debating and such courses as economics and sociology is evident, but debating sometimes helps in subjects farther afield. An English class studying Benét's *John Brown's Body* happened to include a debater. The instructor mentioned that Benét had a reputation for historical accuracy. The debater decided to find out whether it was justified. He selected as the subject of his term paper the references made by Benét to the city of Washington.

He spent his Christmas vacation in the Library of Congress, the Federal Archives Building, newspaper offices, and government offices checking the accuracy of every statement made by Benét about Washington.

When Benét mentioned a drizzly rain, the debater checked the old Weather Bureau records to find the actual precipitation in Washington on the day in question. When Benét mentioned a certain Confederate army sighting the "spires of Washington," the debater checked to find out how close the army actually got to Washington, and whether in those days there were any buildings in the city with spires. When Benét said he was indebted to Walt Whitman's *Specimen Days and Collect* for a description of soldiers pouring back into the city after their defeat, the debater dug out from the Library of Congress an old battered copy of the original Whitman paper to find whether Benét had included in his quotation any details that Whitman had not included in the original. He also checked to find out whether Whitman was in the city on the day in question, or whether he was depending on second-hand information himself. The student attributed his A in the course to this one paper, and he attributed the research to his debate training.

The third immediate return to the debater is in other extracurricular activities. In one high school, where the job of editor-in-chief of the yearbook is considered one of the top school honors, a debater decided that he would do his best to get the job. Each nominee was to be interviewed by a board of three, consisting of the preceding editor-in-chief, the preceding associate editor, and the faculty adviser.

The debater knew better than to face such an interview unprepared. He reasoned that he should spend as much time and effort preparing for the interview as he would in preparing for a debate, which was considerable. He carefully examined the last three yearbooks and brought a copy of the latest one with him to the interview. When questioned, he mentioned that he thought certain improvements could be made, and was asked to explain. His explanation showed the amount of research and thinking he had done. He got the job.

Later in the year, the faculty adviser told him that the board had been hesitating between him and one other student, but the interview determined their action. The debater believes that his success in the interview was due to his debate training.

In another case, a high school debater joined a club composed of about sixty persons, largely non-debaters, devoted to the study of current national problems. He was elected vice president at the second meeting he attended, largely as a result of his contributions to the first meeting. He attributed this to his debate training.

These, then, are some immediate returns to the debater: personal enjoyment in participation, help in academic work, and help in other extracurricular activities.

NATIONAL DEBATE TOPICS AND TOURNAMENT WINNERS

NATIONAL HIGH SCHOOL TOPICS

National debate topics used by high schools appear below.[1] The topics are chosen each year by the NUEA state leagues and the NFL.

1927-8   Resolved, that a federal department of education should be created with a secretary in the President's cabinet.

1928-9   Resolved, that the English cabinet method of legislation is more efficient than the committee system is in the United States.

1929-30   Resolved, that installment buying of personal property as now practiced in the United States is both socially and economically desirable.

1930-1   Resolved, that chain stores are detrimental to the best interests of the American public.

1931-2   Resolved, that the several states should enact legislation providing for compulsory unemployment insurance.

1932-3   Resolved, that at least one half of all state and local revenues should be derived from sources other than tangible property.

1933-4   Resolved, that the United States should adopt the essential features of the British system of radio control and operation.

1934-5   Resolved, that the federal government should adopt the policy of equalizing educational opportunity throughout the nation by means of annual grants to the several states for public elementary and secondary education.

[1] The topics from 1928 to 1950 are published in *The National Forensic League, 1925-1950*, issued by the League in 1950. Many other interesting historical facts are included in this fine anniversary volume.

1935-6   Resolved, that the several states should enact legislation providing for a system of complete medical service available to all citizens at public expense.

1936-7   Resolved, that all electric utilities should be governmentally owned and operated.

1937-8   Resolved, that the several states should adopt a unicameral system of legislation.

1938-9   Resolved, that the United States should establish an alliance with Great Britain.

1939-40   Resolved, that the federal government should own and operate the railroads.

1940-1   Resolved, that the power of the federal government should be increased.

1941-2   Resolved, that every able-bodied male citizen in the United States should be required to have one year of full-time military training before attaining the present draft age.

1942-3   Resolved, that a federal world government should be established.

1943-4   Resolved, that the United States should join in reconstituting the League of Nations.

1944-5   Resolved, that the legal voting age should be reduced to eighteen years.

1945-6   Resolved, that every able-bodied male citizen of the United States should have one year of full-time military training before attaining age 24.

1946-7   Resolved, that the federal government should provide a system of complete medical care available to all citizens at public expense.

1947-8   Resolved, that the federal government should require arbitration of labor disputes in all basic American industries.

1948-9   Resolved, that the United Nations now be revised into a federal world government.

1949-50   Resolved, that the President of the United States should be elected by a direct vote of the people.

1950-1   Resolved, that the American people should reject the welfare state.

1951-2   Resolved, that every American citizen should be subject to conscription for essential service in time of war.

1952-3   Resolved, that the Atlantic pact nations should form a federal union.

1953-4   Resolved, that the President of the United States should be elected by a direct vote of the people.

1954-5   Resolved, that the federal government should initiate a policy of free trade among nations friendly to the United States.

1955-6   Resolved, that governmental subsidies should be granted according to need to high school graduates who qualify for additional training.

National College Topics

The national intercollegiate topic was born in 1920.[2] From 1920 until 1938, the topic was chosen solely by Pi Kappa Delta; other schools readily accepted it because of the convenience it offered when arranging trips and tournaments.

The Mid-West Conference is known to have selected a topic of its own for some years, not always the same as the national topic. One former midwest debater recalls debating four sides of two questions in successive one-night stands during the 1927-1931 period. It is possible that other conferences also selected their own topics.

Since 1938, the national topic has been chosen by the SAA (Speech Association of America) Committee on Intercollegiate Debate and Discussion Activities, and its predecessors under different names. The committee is composed of one representative each from Pi Kappa Delta, Delta Sigma Rho, Tau Kappa Alpha, Phi Rho Pi, American Forensic Association, and Speech Association of America. The chairmanship rotates among the six members.[3]

[2] D. J. Nabors' research among the early issues of *Forensic* indicates that one of the originators of the proposal was J. R. Macarthur in the Spring of 1919. In October 1919, Charles A. Marsh, National Secretary of PKD, asked chapters for suggestions for a national topic for the following year. Nine responded. The selection was made by referendum among the chapters.

[3] For details, see Larry Norton's "Report of the 1955 National Questions Committee," *Forensic*, 41:23-4, October 1955.

National topics to date are listed below.[4]

1920-1   (Men) Resolved, that a progressive tax on land
should be adopted in the United States.
(Men) Resolved, that the League of Nations
should be adopted.
(Women) Resolved, that intercollegiate athletics
should be abolished.

1921-2   Resolved, that the principle of the "closed shop" is
unjustifiable.

1922-3   Resolved, that the United States should adopt the
cabinet-parliamentary form of government.

1923-4   Resolved, that the United States should enter the
World Court of the League of Nations as proposed
by President Harding.

1924-5   Resolved, that Congress should be empowered to
override by a two-thirds vote decisions of the Supreme Court which declare acts of Congress unconstitutional.

1925-6   (Men) Resolved, that the constitution of the United
States should be amended to give Congress power
to regulate child labor.
(Women) Resolved, that the United States should
adopt a uniform marriage and divorce law.

1926-7   (Men) Resolved, that the essential features of the
McNary-Haugen bill be enacted into law.
(Women) Resolved, that trial by jury should be
abolished.

1927-8   Resolved, that the United States should cease to
protect, by force of arms, capital invested in foreign lands, except after formal declaration of war.

1928-9   Resolved, that a substitute for trial by jury should
be adopted.

[4] Official Pi Kappa Delta topics were compiled by D. J. Nabors, National
Secretary-Treasurer, from PKD records. In a few instances where exact wording is in doubt, reference was made to E. R. Nichols' "The Annual College
Debate Question," *Debater's Magazine*, 3:206-7, December 1947, and other un-
official sources. While there are several minor conflicts in wording between various sources, the only really substantial difference is for the year 1926-7. Nichols
gives, "Resolved, that the Volstead Act should be modified to permit the manufacture and sales of light wines and beer."

1929-30 Resolved, that the nations should adopt a plan of complete disarmament, excepting such forces as are needed for police purposes.

1930-1 Resolved, that the nations should adopt a policy of free trade.

1931-2 Resolved, that Congress should enact legislation providing for the centralized control of industry.

1932-3 Resolved, that the Allied war debts should be canceled.

1933-4 Resolved, that the powers of the President of the United States should be substantially increased as a settled policy.

1934-5 Resolved, that the nations should agree to prevent the international shipment of arms and munitions.

1935-6 Resolved, that Congress should have the power to override, by a two-thirds majority vote, decisions of the Supreme Court declaring laws passed by Congress unconstitutional.

1936-7 Resolved, that Congress should be empowered to fix minimum wages and maximum hours for industry.

1937-8 Resolved, that the National Labor Relations Board should be empowered to enforce arbitration of all industrial disputes.

1938-9 Resolved, that the United States should cease to use public funds (including credits) for the purpose of stimulating business.

1939-40 Resolved, that the United States should follow a policy of strict economic and military isolation toward all nations outside the Western Hemisphere engaged in armed international or civil conflict.

1940-1 Resolved, that the nations of the Western Hemisphere should form a permanent union.

1941-2 Resolved, that the federal government should regulate by law all labor unions in the United States.

1942-3 Resolved, that the United States should take the initiative in establishing a permanent federal union with power to tax and regulate commerce, to settle international disputes and to enforce such settlements, to maintain a police force, and to provide for the admission of other nations which accept the principles of the union.

1943-4 Resolved, that the United States should cooperate in establishing and maintaining an international police force upon the defeat of the Axis.

1944-5 Resolved, that the federal government should enact legislation requiring the settlement of all labor disputes by compulsory arbitration when voluntary means of settlement have failed.

1945-6 Resolved, that the policy of the United States should be directed toward the establishment of free trade among the nations of the world.

1946-7 Resolved, that labor should be given a direct share in the management of industry.

1947-8 Resolved, that a federal world government should be established.

1948-9 Resolved, that the federal government should adopt a policy of equalizing educational opportunity in tax supported schools by means of annual grants.

1949-50 Resolved, that the United States should nationalize the basic non-agricultural industries.

1950-1 Resolved, that non-communist nations should form a new international organization.

1951-2 Resolved, that the federal government should adopt a permanent program of wage and price control.

1952-3 Resolved, that the Congress of the United States should enact a compulsory Fair Employment Practices Law.

1953-4 Resolved, that the United States should adopt a policy of free trade.

1954-5 Resolved, that the United States should extend diplomatic recognition to the Communist government of China.

1955-6 Resolved, that the non-agricultural industries should guarantee their employees an annual wage.

1956-7 Resolved, that the United States should discontinue direct economic aid to foreign countries.

ALTERNATIVE TOPICS

As can be seen from the above lists, the affirmative is often expected to recommend "social legislation" or increased governmental activity. Since both major political parties currently advocate similar activities, the national topics are not always of great interest.

To secure a better clash, some schools select their own topics. It is effective, for instance, to select a topic in which the affirmative supports action *away* from, rather than towards, such positions. The 1956-57 college topic is an excellent example.

Interesting and controversial debates may be held on topics such as these:

International

Resolved, that the United States should withdraw diplomatic recognition of the U.S.S.R. and its satellites.

Resolved, that the United States should withdraw from the United Nations.

Resolved, that the United States Constitution should be amended to provide that a provision of a treaty or other international agreement which conflicts with any provision of the Constitution shall not be of any force or effect.

Free enterprise versus *government control*

Resolved, that all forms of public interstate transportation should be given equivalent treatment with regard to regulations, taxes, and subsidies.

Resolved, that the railroads should be granted substantially greater freedom to establish rates for their services.

Resolved, that private business should be permitted to compete with the Post Office in the carrying of mail.

Resolved, that the federal government should abolish agricultural price supports.

Governmental efficiency

Resolved, that civilian employees of the federal government should be promptly decreased in number by at least 50 per cent.

Resolved, that peacetime income, gift, and inheritance taxes for individuals and businesses should be limited to a maximum of 25 per cent.

Resolved, that the federal government should substantially strengthen its internal security program.

Labor

Resolved, that the federal government should enact legislation providing that no person shall be prevented from gaining or holding employment because of membership or lack of membership in a labor organization.

Resolved, that labor unions should not be permitted to represent the employees of more than one company.

Resolved, that labor unions should be subject to the provisions of antitrust laws governing businesses.

NATIONAL HIGH SCHOOL TOURNAMENT WINNERS

The winners of the National Forensic League's annual tournament are generally recognized as the national high school debating champions for the year. Winners have been:

1930-1 First: Miami, Oklahoma
        Second: Topeka, Kansas

1931-2 First: Omaha-North HS, Nebraska
        Second: Rapid City, South Dakota

1932-3 First: Altus, Oklahoma
        Second: Hutchinson, Kansas

1933-4 First: Oklahoma City-Central HS, Oklahoma
        Second: Elgin, Illinois

1934-5 First: Sioux Falls, South Dakota
Second: Los Angeles HS, California
1935-6 First: Duquoin, Illinois
Second: Carrollton, Missouri
1936-7 First: Oklahoma City-Classen HS, Oklahoma
Second: Elgin, Illinois
1937-8 First: Elgin, Illinois
Second: Seminole, Oklahoma
1938-9 First: Oklahoma City-Classen HS, Oklahoma
Second: Bristow, Oklahoma
1939-40 First: Bristow, Oklahoma
Second: Sioux City-East HS, Iowa
1940-1 First: Oklahoma City-Classen HS, Oklahoma
Second: Burlington, Iowa
1949-50 First: Dallas-Adamson HS, Texas
Second: Oklahoma City-Marshall HS, Oklahoma
1950-1 First: Oklahoma City-Classen HS, Oklahoma
Second: Seminole, Oklahoma
1951-2 First: Shreveport-Byrd HS, Louisiana
Second: Chaminade, New York
1952-3 First: Pueblo-Centennial HS, Colorado
Second: Edmond, Oklahoma
1953-4 First: Miami Beach, Florida
Second: Louisville, Ohio
1954-5 First: Miami Senior HS, Florida
Second: Seminole, Oklahoma
1955-6 First: Seminole, Oklahoma
Second: South St. Paul, Minnesota

National College Tournament Winners

The winners of the West Point Invitational Tournament
are generally recognized as the national college champions
for that year. Results to date have been:

1946-7 First: Southeastern State College (Oklahoma)
Second: University of Southern California
1947-8 First: North Texas State Teachers College
Second: University of Florida

1948-9 First: University of Alabama
       Second: Baylor University
1949-50 First: University of Vermont
       Second: Augustana College
1950-1 First: University of Redlands
       Second: De Pauw University
1951-2 First: University of Redlands
       Second: Baylor University
1952-3 First: University of Miami
       Second: College of the Holy Cross
1953-4 First: University of Kansas
       Second: University of Florida
1954-5 First: University of Alabama
       Second: Wilkes College
1955-6 First: United States Military Academy
       Second: St. Joseph's College

APPENDIX C

BIBLIOGRAPHY

Books: High School Debate Texts

Three books which are especially suitable for high school debaters, yet which also have value in college work, are listed below:

Holm, James N., *Successful Discussion and Debate.* Portland 1, Maine. J. Weston Walch. Annual. $2

> This handy paper-bound volume is a cross between a high school text and debate handbook. Revised annually, it gives many current examples in its review of debating techniques.

Quimby, Brooks, *So You Want to Discuss and Debate!* Portland 1, Maine. J. Weston Walch. 1955. $2

> This is another paper-bound volume, published by the same organization. Written by a true master of the subject, it contains a wealth of practical advice. The chapter on cross examination is, in the opinion of this reviewer, unexcelled in debate literature; it deserves careful study by both high school and college debaters.

> Both books are written in an interesting, non-technical style, using the second person. Readers interested primarily in debate need not fear the title of either book.

Summers, Harrison Boyd; Whan, Forest Livings; and Rousse, Thomas Andrew, *How to Debate.* 3d edition. H. W. Wilson Company. New York. 1950. $3

> For some years now, this has been recognized as a sound, practical book, pointed primarily toward beginners. It is not specifically designated for high school use, but it is ideally suited for that field.

> The reader will find a good foundation on which to build. The fact that the book is now in its third edition is ample evidence of its acceptance throughout the country.

Books: College Debate Texts

The selection of a worth-while text for classroom use will depend largely on the goals of the course. The texts listed below are pointed toward competitive debate, and are currently available.

One of the most important qualifications for a good text —other than competence in subject matter—is that it be written for the student. This is not easy. It means writing in clear language, with clear organization, and sticking to the subject.

The final test of any text is how well it does the job for which it is to be used.

Courtney, Luther W., and Capp, Glenn R., *Practical Debating.* Philadelphia. J. B. Lippincott Company. 1949. $3.50

The authors have done well in naming this book. Drawing from a wealth of experience, they have emphasized debate as they have taught it to many highly successful teams.

Crocker, Lionel, *Argumentation and Debate.* New York. American Book Company. 1944. $4.25

This is a widely respected text, competently written by a man who knows his subject, and who has the ability to make it clear to his readers. There are numerous illustrations bridging the gap between classroom work and post-graduation activities.

Although written in 1944, it remains one of the most valuable texts on contest debating currently in print.

Potter, David, ed., *Argumentation and Debate.* New York. Dryden Press. 1954. $5

This is the most recent text on contest debating. Under the able editorship of David Potter, twenty-five teachers have contributed the articles that comprise the book. There is a refreshing emphasis, throughout, on intercollegiate debating as it actually exists.

Books: Supplemental Reading

The following books provide much interesting and instructive background material. They are not listed as debate texts because of their emphasis on allied subjects (discussion, nature and forms of argument, logic, briefing, and parliamentary procedure). However, most of these books do contain material on contest debating. All are currently in print.

Baird, A. Craig, *Argumentation, Discussion and Debate.* New York. McGraw-Hill Book Company. 1950. $4.50
Four chapters are devoted to debate, covering principles, refutation, special types, and judging.

Behl, William A., *Discussion and Debate: An Introduction to Argument.* New York. Ronald Press. 1953. $4
The author makes clear his view that while debate and discussion are different, they have much in common. His chapter on "Topics for Argument" is especially valuable.

The book is written in clear, simple language. A number of illustrations from actual debates are included.

The chapter on "Exposing Obstacles to Clear Thinking" helpfully describes refutation in terms of actual practice, and warns against any attempt to use formal fallacies in logic for this purpose.

Interestingly enough, Professor Behl makes use of the "advantage-disadvantage" type of analysis in his chapter on "Types of Debate," which will appeal to those who are using similar analyses in their debate cases.

The book also includes material on formal logic, preparing the brief, discussion methods, types of discussion, and other material primarily of background interest to the debater.

Braden, Waldo Warder, *Oral Decision Making: Principles of Discussion and Debate.* New York. Harper & Brothers. 1955. $4.75
As the title indicates, this fine book is pointed toward the general field of oral decisions in various forms.

One of the highlights, from the debater's standpoint, is the chapter on "Answering Arguments," which is discussed in a very helpful and practical manner.

Chenoweth, Eugene C., *Discussion and Debate.* Dubuque, Iowa. William C. Brown Company. 1951. $2.95
Professor Chenoweth's approach, appropriately enough, is that of a teacher. He writes in the second person, just as though he were in conference with a student. It is a commendable plan.

While only a relatively small portion of the book is devoted to debate as such, much worth-while information is included on those pages. Part V, "Extracurricular Forensics," is especially valuable.

Ewbank, Henry Lee, and Auer, J. Jeffrey, *Discussion and Debate: Tools of a Democracy.* 2d edition. New York. Appleton-Century-Crofts. 1951. $4

Part V, on debate, is a welcome addition to the literature of the subject. The chapter on "Nature and Purposes of Debate" is especially refreshing in refuting some common misconceptions held by those who should know better.

The authors are close to their subject and speak from a wealth of experience.

Gulley, Halbert E., *Essentials of Discussion and Debate.* New York. Henry Holt & Company. 1955. $1.50

This is a handy, paper-bound pocket manual, written for either high school or college use, but especially suited for high schools. As the title indicates, it sticks to the essentials. It is useful in stating first principles clearly and concisely.

Approximately half of the book is devoted to debate.

- McBurney, James H., O'Neill, James M., and Mills, Glenn E., *Argumentation and Debate: Techniques of a Free Society.* Macmillan Company. 1951. $4

This is a scholarly work, of especial appeal to instructors and graduate students. Considerable interesting background material on the nature and types of argument is included.

A feature of particular interest to debaters is a transcript of the 1948 debate between Dewey and Stassen on the question, "Should the Communist Party in the United States be Outlawed?"

Wellman, Francis L., *The Art of Cross-Examination.* 4th edition. New York. Macmillan Company. 1951. $5

Written primarily for lawyers, this fascinating book illustrates many principles useful to debaters. The author shows, for instance, how effective it is to confront the witness with inconsistencies while he is still on the stand, and how the point can be dulled if the examiner waits until summary, by which time the answers have been half forgotten and the significance lost.

Somewhat over half of the book is devoted to famous cross examinations, which are both reproduced and explained.

Books: Reference Material On Debate Topics

Reference Shelf. New York. H. W. Wilson Company. $2 per volume, $8 per year for six volumes.

Some of the best known and most widely used reference books are those in the *Reference Shelf*. Each of the six volumes contains background reading on a current issue; the debater who fails to read this material is not in an enviable position. Titles, of course, vary but one issue is always devoted to the high school topic.

Carpenter, Oliver C., *Debate Outlines on Public Questions.* 8th edition. Mail and Express Publishing Company. 160 Varick Street. New York. 1947. $3

The appeal of this book through eight editions can readily be understood when one uses it. The author is a practicing New York attorney. Thirty-five topics are covered, with a bibliography and brief for each. The subjects are remarkably well chosen. Even though this edition was published in 1947, most of the material promises to remain fresh and debatable for some time to come. College squads looking for topics to debate, other than the annual national topic, will find this book an excellent source of ideas.

Handbooks: High School

Annual handbooks for high school debaters are published by the organizations listed below.

Although all are devoted to the national high school topic, there is surprisingly little duplication. The authors present different viewpoints and facts. The debater who wishes to prepare thoroughly should study them all. The budget of the debate squad may well be set up with that in mind.

In some instances, it is possible to purchase (say) five books of a kind at a reduced price. Where the squad is large, it is worth while to take advantage of such offers.

Mid-West Debate Bureau, P.O. Box 8, Normal, Illinois. Harold E. Gibson, director.

Debate Handbook, $3.35

This fine annual paper-bound volume covers about 250 pages. It consists of a lesson series covering nine or ten phases of the national high school topic, together with bibliography, briefs, rebuttal files, sample dilemmas, and other features.

Format, as well as content, is excellent. It is clear, readable, and helpful.

Debate Review, $2.25

Since the final wording of the high school topic is not announced until about January 1, this January manual serves a very useful purpose. It brings the facts up to date, and considers the exact wording of the final topic.

It is paper-bound, about 100 pages in length.

Your Guide to Effective Rebuttals, $1.75

This is another 100-page paper-bound manual. It is a handbook supplement, devoted to refutation of the standard arguments on the national high school topic.

Set of Speeches, $1.50

This is a set of four speeches on the high school topic. It is not expected that the speeches could be used in actual debate. Rather, they give the inexperienced debater some idea of how the facts can be put together in a talk.

National University Extension Association, Committee on Discussion and Debate Materials. Bower Aly, handbook editor. Robert H. Schacht, 1327 University Avenue, Madison 5, Wisconsin, committee chairman.

Discussion and Debate Manual, two volumes, $3.12

These printed, paper-bound manuals are widely distributed among high school leagues. The first volume is usually devoted to articles prepared especially for this purpose by various authors, while the second volume consists of reprints of articles published elsewhere. For the most part, the manuals are devoted to background material.

Forensic Library, price varies

Each year the committee arranges to obtain a quantity of books and pamphlets related to the national high school topic. In some cases, the material is donated to the committee and in other cases, the price is reduced. The committee, in turn, sells this material to schools and interested individuals. The price varies from year to year, depending on the contents of the package. In a typical recent year, the complete package sold for $11.

Marquette Debaters, Marquette University, 625 North 15th Street, Milwaukee 3, Wisconsin. Hugo Hellman, Director.

Background Books, $3.50, two for $6, four for $10.

This is one of the best series of paper-bound manuals. Its primary emphasis is on facts and reasoning. Each volume drives right to the heart of the subject. It is a "must" for high school debaters.

Walch, J. Weston, publisher, P.O. Box 1075, Portland 1, Maine.

Debate Handbook, $3

This fine paper-backed manual consists of about 200 pages. Included are affirmative and negative briefs and evidence. The strong feature of the book is the extensive annotated bibliography. Facts are given in considerable detail and solidly documented.

The author is long experienced in this field, and he knows how to prepare useful material.

HANDBOOKS: COLLEGE

An annual college handbook on the national college topic is published by:

Mid-West Debate Bureau, P.O. Box 8, Normal, Illinois. Harold E. Gibson, director.

Debate Handbook, $3.35

Paper-bound, this manual consists of about 200 pages, packed with information on the national college topic. Sections are devoted to a lesson series, briefs, affirmative and negative files, strategy, an Authorities Who's Who, and a report on the results of a questionnaire sent to noted authorities. Fallacies and dilemmas are illustrated.

This handbook is a fruitful source of facts and ideas. It is deservedly popular among college debaters.

PERIODICALS: DEBATE

Forensic

Pi Kappa Delta. Editor, Emmett Long, Pepperdine College, Los Angeles, California. Secretary-Treasurer, D. J. Nabors, East Central State College, Ada, Oklahoma. 4 issues per year, each about 34 pages. $1 per year, $2.50 for three years.

Articles of current forensic interest. Debate techniques, chapter and tournament news.

Gavel

Delta Sigma Rho. Editor and Secretary, John W. Keltner, Kansas State College, Manhattan, Kansas. 4 issues per year, each about 32 pages. $1.50 per year.

Articles of current forensic interest. Debate techniques, chapter news.

Persuader

Phi Rho Pi. Editor, Glenn L. Jones, 1171 Garrison Street, Denver 15, Colorado. 3 issues per year, each about 6 pages in newspaper form.

Primarily chapter news.

Rostrum

National Forensic League. Secretary, Bruno Jacob, Ripon, Wisconsin. 9 issues per year, each about 16 pages. $1 per year.

News of high school debating and the NFL tournament. Debate techniques.

Speaker

Tau Kappa Alpha. Editor, Victor M. Powell, Wabash College, Crawfordsville, Indiana. 4 issues per year, each about 36 pages. $1 per year, $5 for life.

Articles of current forensic interest. Debate techniques, chapter news.

PERIODICALS: GENERAL REFERENCE MATERIAL

Congressional Digest

1631 K Street NW, Washington 6, D.C. 10 issues per year. $7 per year.

Pro and con articles on questions of current interest, mostly by congressional and government leaders. Not a United States Government publication.

Editorial Research Reports

1011 20th Street NW, Washington, D.C. Weekly.

Documented reports on matters of current public interest.

PERIODICALS: OPINION

In addition to the standard general magazines and news magazines, debaters will find much useful material in the journals of opinion.

Politically, these magazines are to the left or the right of the middle of the road, and they are often frankly partisan, but they are valuable for precisely that reason. They are not afraid to carry their arguments to the limit, and are not afraid to make enemies. They often give names, dates, places, examples—just the sort of information debaters thrive on.

Right of center: Articles advocating limited government and a free economy; against government intervention in economic affairs; against communism and socialism; generally in sympathy with the right wing of the Republican party and with conservative Democrats.

American Mercury

250 West 57th Street, New York 19. Monthly. $4 per year.

Freeman

Irvington-On-Hudson, New York. Monthly. $5 per year.

National Review

211 East 37th Street, New York 16. Weekly. $7 per year.

Left of center: Articles favoring a strong hand by the federal government in economic matters; generally in sympathy with the Roosevelt New Deal, the Truman Fair Deal, and the left wing of the Democratic party.

Nation

333 Sixth Avenue, New York 14. Weekly. $7 per year.

New Republic

1826 Jefferson Place NW, Washington 6, D.C. Weekly. $7 per year.

Reporter

136 East 57th Street, New York 22. Bi-weekly. $5 per year.

MAGAZINE ARTICLES: THE WELLS-O'NEILL CONTROVERSY

The debater or coach who desires an evening of fascinating reading could do worse than consult the first four volumes of the *Quarterly Journal of Speech,* published at the time of World War I.

It seems that Professors O'Neill, Davis, Sarett, and Wells were not in complete agreement on the manner in which debates should be judged, and their verbal slugging match extended over a period of three years.

The articles make enjoyable reading, not only because they contribute so much to our understanding of the principles of debate judging today, but also because the participants possessed a subtle sense of humor which crops out again and again in their arguments.

All of the following references are to the *Quarterly Journal of Public Speaking,* now known as the *Quarterly Journal of Speech.*

O'Neill, James Milton, "A Disconcerted Editor and Others," 1:79-84, April 1915.

Davis, William Hawley, "Debating as Related to Non-Academic Life," 1:105-13, July 1915.

O'Neill, "Able Non-Debaters," 1:201-5, July 1915.

O'Neill, "Judges Again," 1:305-7, October 1915.

Davis, "Is Debating Primarily a Game?" 2:171-9, April 1916.

O'Neill, "Game or Counterfeit Presentment," 2:193-7, April 1916.

Sarett, Lew R., "The Expert Judge of Debate," 3:135-9, April 1917.

Wells, Hugh Neal, "Judging Debates," 3:336-45, October 1917.

O'Neill, "The Juryman's Vote in Debate," 3:346-55, October 1917.

Wells, "Judging Debates, I," 4:76-83, January 1918.

O'Neill, "Judging Debates, II," 4:83-6, January 1918.

Wells, "Judging Debates, III," 4:86-91, January 1918.

O'Neill, "Judging Debates, IV," 4:91-2, January 1918.

Wells, "Coaching Debates," 4:170-83, March 1918.

Wells, "A Final Reply," 4:398-409, October 1918.

O'Neill, "Comment on Judge Wells' Last Ms.," 4:410-21, October 1918.

Wells, "Comment on Professor O'Neill's Last Ms.," 4:422-7, October 1918.

Sarett, "A Juryman-Critic's Vote," 4:428-33, October 1918.

Magazine Articles: Recent

Many interesting and helpful articles on debate have been published in recent years. Some of them are listed below.

Boyle, Karl, "It's Invigorating," *Rostrum,* 30:4:5, December 1955.

Cross-question debate is invigorating and challenging to the debaters. The important issues are faced, and there is clear indication of the debater's skills in analysis, adaptation, extempore speaking, and development of sound evidence.

Brandes, Paul Dickerson, "A Public Relations Program for Debate," *Speaker,* 35:10-14, March 1953.

The author recommends a strong promotional program for debate. He suggests, among other things, letters to parents of debaters, letters to alumni, an alumni luncheon at Homecoming, letters to people thanking them for services rendered, news stories and photographs, a few highly publicized audience debates on issues of local concern, publicity for beginning debaters, advice from faculty members, quick replies to invitations, telegrams of good wishes to tournaments if unable to attend, and ownership of a camera.

Capp, Glenn R., "Debating the Affirmative," *Forensic,* 40: 44-7, January 1955.

The task of the affirmative is analyzed.

Carmack, Paul A., "Survey of Forensic Finances," *Speech Activities,* 7:5-7, Spring 1951.

A survey was taken for the American Forensic Association of 112 colleges and universities. Budgets ranged from $25 to $3600. The forensic staff, in most cases, consisted of two people. The number of debates ranged from 40 to 200. The average cost per debate ranged from $8.70 in the East to $13.00 in the West. These figures were obtained by dividing each school's total yearly debate budget by the number of debates held.

Ewbank, Henry Lee, "What's Right with Debate," *Quarterly Journal of Speech,* 37:197-202, April 1951.

The author offers some interesting observations and evidence on the value of debate.

He reports that of the 5500 members of Delta Sigma Rho who graduated before 1928, about 11 per cent are listed in "Who's Who in America."

The group includes 53 college or university presidents, 25 judges (two of them members of the United States Supreme Court), 45 United States senators, representatives, or governors, and numerous business executives and leaders in other fields.

Freeley, Austin J., "A Survey of College Forensics," *Gavel,* 33:50-2, March 1951.

An analysis of the forensic programs of twenty-six colleges and universities in various parts of the country shows that during the 1949-1950 season, budgets ranged from $400 to $8200, with an average of $2010. The number of debates ranged from 10 to 125, with an average of 39. Interesting comparisons are made between schools with good records and those with poor records.

Hance, Kenneth, "The Dialectic Method in Debate," *Quarterly Journal of Speech,* 25:243-8, April 1939.

Greek philosophers' ideas can be applied to modern Oregon style debating. Among the author's conclusions are these:

"The cross questioning may concern itself with either the arguments of the opponent or those of the questioner, the purpose in either case being the establishment of conclusions pertinent to the argument at hand.

"The questioner should ask specific and unequivocal questions— those requiring a 'yes' or 'no' answer or a short reply. The questioner should protect himself carefully at this point, and should control the amount of time devoted to the consideration of each question."

Hargis, Donald E., "A Note on Championship Debaters," *Quarterly Journal of Speech,* 34:57-8, February 1948.

A study was made of high school debaters—who they were, what they did in high school, and what happened to them after graduation. The results are in this article.

Hellman, Hugo E., "Debating is Debating—and Should Be," *Quarterly Journal of Speech*, 31:295-300, October 1945.

The author pricks some balloons by pointing out that students, after graduation, will be faced with opponents who are not always idealistic, and that in many cases the question is not, "How are we going to get an occupant for the White House?" but "Shall it be X or Y?" He concludes that debate is excellent training for such situations.

Lambertson, F. W., "Plan and Counterplan in a Question of Policy," *Quarterly Journal of Speech*, 29:48-52, February 1943.

How much of a detailed "plan in action" must an affirmative team present?

When judging debates, the author was troubled with that problem. In some debates the affirmative would show that evils existed and would then suggest that the plan would work and had benefits. All of the time the author kept wondering, "What plan?"

In order to find out, he sent a questionnaire to a number of his colleagues. The results are reported in this article. Among the comments quoted are these:

"I think the affirmative is obligated to present a plan that is sufficiently detailed to demonstrate the plan's workability."—Ray K. Immel.

"The affirmative should present a plan sufficiently detailed to give reasonable evidence that the proposal would, if adopted, be feasible—workable."—P. L. Soper.

The author also asked opinions regarding counterplans. He concluded:

"A counterplan must involve a change of principle from that of the proposition. No change of principle, no counterplan."

Lambertson, F. W., "The Meaning of the Word 'Should' in a Question of Policy," *Quarterly Journal of Speech*, 28: 421-4, December 1942.

Concerned with the "could-should-would" problem, the author undertook to find out what forensic directors and leaders in the speech field thought. This article gives the results.

Lambertson gives as his own conclusion the opinion of Ray K. Immel:

"The only question at issue is, would the plan probably improve conditions, or would it probably not? On the answer to that simple question, the debate should be decided. Would we gain more than we would lose or would we lose more than we would gain by adopting the affirmative plan?"

The author points out that the problem-solver cannot evade reality here; he must suggest the nature of his remedy and show how he proposes to put it into operation.

Immel continues:

"If the negative can show that because of overwhelming opposition the plan could not be made to work, I should say that the negative would be justified in using that argument; but it would not be an argument against any measure merely to say that you cannot get enough votes to pass it."

Alan Nichols' opinion is essentially the same:

"A policy should be adopted if its adoption will result in more benefits than evils."

The author concludes that the word "should" includes the word "could." Whether or not Congress or the people "would" adopt a particular reform at the present time is beside the point.

Legere, Lawrence J., Jr., "The West Point Debate Tournament," *Quarterly Journal of Speech*, 32:54-6, February 1948.

The founding of the national college invitational tournament is described.

Long, Emmett T., "Rebuttal Technique," *Forensic*, 40:50-1, January 1955.

Good rebuttal technique is discussed.

McLaughlin, T. J., "Ethics in Contest Debating," *Speech Activities*, 8:9-10, Spring 1952.

There is general agreement on ethics in debate. This article reports the trend of opinion, based on a study of fourteen texts.

Murphy, Jack W., "A New Look for Debate," *Speaker*, 38:1:3-19, November 1955.

The author suggests several innovations in debate procedure: A round-table seating arrangement; a pre-debate statement by the judge as to what he considers good debating; a time-out during the first affirmative speech for the purpose of determining whether the teams agree on the definitions; a time-out if a debater believes he is being misquoted or misinterpreted; and an over-all longer time allowance for the debate.

Musgrave, George M., "The Double-Summary Technique in Debate," *Quarterly Journal of Speech*, 32:458-68, December 1946.

Double-summary methods are useful both in case organization and in judging.

Musgrave, George M., "Organization of Debate Cases," *Forensic*, 34:7-9, October 1948.

The author gives some of the history of the brief type of case organization, and offers the advantage-disadvantage technique as a modern alternative especially designed for the proposition of policy.

Musgrave, George M., "Radio Debate at M.I.T.," *Debater's Magazine*, 2:158-61, September 1946.

M.I.T.'s first experience with radio debate began during the war. The Colonial Network assigned good radio time: a full hour broadcast over 20 or 25 stations throughout New England once every two weeks.

To produce debates of audience interest, Oregon 6-5-5 timing was used. To make it easy for the radio audience to distinguish between teams, M.I.T. debated girls' schools where possible, but this was limited by the number of well qualified girls' teams in the vicinity, and it was finally necessary to give up the idea.

A sizable student staff was necessary to manage the program; it was entirely student-run.

It was, of course, necessary to debate a different topic every second week. The top eight debaters were assigned primarily to radio debates to allow sufficient time for preparation of so many different topics.

Critic judges were employed, and were asked to come to the microphone immediately after the final rebuttal to give the decision and the reasons for it. This system was found to operate well, and not work too much of a hardship on the judge.

During the war the debaters had to be extremely careful of controversial remarks on international topics; some of the things that happened make interesting reading.

Nichols, Egbert Ray, "Historical Sketch of Intercollegiate Debating," *Speech Activities*, 8:5-32, Spring 1952.

This is an interesting account of intercollegiate debate from its beginnings to the present day. For convenience, the author has divided the time into decades, and has brought out the important developments of each decade.

Nichols, Egbert Ray, "Our Trip to Japan," *Speech Activities*, 9:88-91, Winter 1953.

Upon his retirement as head of the Department of Speech, University of Redlands, Professor Nichols went to Japan to help the growth of the Japanese debating movement. This is one of several articles in which he reported his experiences.

Norton, Larry, "Report of the 1955 National Questions Committee," *Forensic*, 41:23-4, October 1955.

The chairman of the Speech Association of America Committee on Intercollegiate Debate and Discussion Activities gives an interesting factual report on the method of selecting the national college topic.

Quimby, Brooks, "A Rebuttal That Took Thirty Years to Develop," *Speech Activities*, 8:35-7, Summer 1952.

The Bates College chapter of Delta Sigma Rho made a study of the lives of its members. The results were favorable to debate. Some of the evidence is given in this article.

Sillars, Malcolm, "The Counter Plan," *Speech Activities*, 7: 131-2, Winter 1951.

Effective use of the counterplan is discussed. The author suggests that the debater (1) select the plan for the worth of the argument, not trickery, (2) introduce the counterplan in the first negative speech, (3) make his position clear and definite early in the debate, and (4) make the clash between the plans the major issue.

Sillars, Malcolm, "Reexamination of Strategic Debate," *Speech Activities*, 8:10-30, Spring 1952.

The author effectively clears away some misconceptions about debate strategy. He shows that both the good and the bad elements can be exaggerated, and that when the smoke has cleared, true strategy is an integral part of all debating, carrying with it an ethical responsibility.

Sillars, Malcolm, "Summary," *Speech Activities*, 7:44-5, Summer 1951.

The importance of adequate summary in debate is sometimes overlooked. The author has several suggestions: Summarize in every speech. Spend sufficient time in summary. Summarize everything up to date, not just your speech. Summarize in basically the same terms that you used in the body of the speech. Know your case well and use the same number of points in the speech as in the summary.

Westerfield, Hargis, "Decision Debating: A Philosophy," *Quarterly Journal of Speech*, 28:24-7, February 1942.

Decisions—even unfair decisions—are important in making men and women out of high school students.

Westerfield, Hargis, "Mass Debating: Incentives and Techniques," *Quarterly Journal of Speech*, 26:420-6, October 1940.

"Interscholastic debating is as popular as football in central Kentucky. We can safely make this statement, when Winchester, Corbin, and Henry Clay of Lexington report 20 simultaneous debates between opposing schools; and when little Georgetown of 150 pupils announces that 25 active debaters have already carried on 94 contests in six weeks' time. Georgetown's 94 debates with 25 participants have cost $50.53, an average of less than 54 cents per individual contest, half of the total of which was used for debate material and registration fees.

"A specialized Oral English class was found necessary. A full year's credit in English was offered toward graduation, in exchange for any regular year in English excepting the first. Registration for this class has been doubly limited. No more than sixteen students are permitted in it. A "B" average is also prerequisite.

"Rewards for debating are even as high as those of football and basketball! Letters are conferred, just as in athletics, for participation in a certain number of debates. Contestants are often excused from school to travel distances. When Georgetown is host at a debate rally, the entire school enjoys short-period sessions and a half-holiday. The local papers are avid to print this type of news, with due attention to individuals' names."

NFL membership is an incentive for successful debaters.

The season is concluded with a full-time assembly program, including speeches by successful alumni, an exhibition debate, and plenty of applause directed by cheer leaders.

Wilson, O. J., "Techniques for Stimulating Interest in Debate," *Gavel*, 38:11-26, November 1955.

The author's thesis is that any worth-while activity, at any level of education, on any campus, will succeed in direct proportion to the interest of the teacher responsible therefor. He offers a number of helpful, constructive suggestions that have proved successful.

INDEX